Every Wild Voice:

For environmental leaders, both present and future

Sam Davis, Ph.D.

Published in the United States

Independently published, 2024

Although this publication is designed to provide accurate information regarding the subject matter covered, the publisher and the author assume no responsibility for errors, inaccuracies, omissions, or any other inconsistencies herein. This publication is meant as a source of valuable information for the reader, however it is not meant as a replacement for direct expert assistance. If such level of assistance is required, the services of a competent professional should be sought.

To those who have gone before us – we are standing on the shoulders of giants.

In loving memory of Boo, Ramses, Maya, Cyrus, and Bud.

Table of Contents

1 FOREWORD

Your community needs leaders who care about the environment. As climate change, pollution, and loss of biodiversity threaten our planet's health, we can't afford to wait for governments or corporations to solve these problems. We need individuals who are willing to take action, inspire others, and make a difference. And those differences need to happen right in our backyards.

I am a scientist, and I can tell you: scientists aren't always effective. They're more concerned with their careers and publishing papers than they are about applying that knowledge to fixing the world's problems. Or they forget to bring their big models and experiments down to the real world. They don't tell people what it means and why they should care. It's not malicious. But it is benign neglect. And it leaves the rest of us in a bind, acting as a go-between for scientists and policy makers.

Policy makers are often useless, too. They're more interested in holding onto power than solving the urgent problems that their constituents face. A few thousand dollars from a power company helps them turn a blind eye to rising energy costs and over-reliance on fossil fuels. After all, they need that money to be reelected.

That's why we need people like you. You know your community best. You may not know exactly what's in the water, but you know when it looks funny. And, you know where the kids play. You can see right through the political bandying in community meetings to the heart of the issue. Companies and politicians are using your community for their own gain.

Becoming an environmental leader is not easy. It requires knowledge, skills, values, and habits that go beyond recycling, using reusable bags, or turning off lights. It demands a deep understanding of the root causes of environmental issues, the ability to communicate convincingly and inspire action, the courage to challenge the status quo, and the resilience to overcome obstacles and failures.

This book is about how to cultivate environmental leadership in yourself and in others. It draws on research, examples, and stories from various fields, including environmental science, psychology, education, and activism. It offers practical strategies, activities, and reflections that can help you develop and enhance your leadership potential, regardless of your background or experience.

Whether you're a student who wants to ignite a green movement on campus, a professional who wants to integrate sustainability into your work, a parent who wants to raise eco-conscious children, or a citizen who wants to influence policy makers, this book provides a roadmap for you. It shows that leadership is not a fixed trait, but a continuous learning process that can be fostered and shared. It invites you to join the growing community of environmental leaders who are shaping the future of our planet.

In this first part of the book, we'll explore how to "find your why" and figure out what your version of an environmental leadership path looks like. In later parts of this book, we'll explore how you can gather knowledge, apply what you've learned, and grow as a leader in your community. Let's get started!

What motivates you to care about the environment? What drives you to take action, make sacrifices, and overcome obstacles for the sake of nature? What is your why for environmental advocacy?

These are not easy questions to answer. For many people, environmental advocacy is not their primary career or identity. It's something they do on the side, out of passion or responsibility. They might recycle, participate in cleanups, sign petitions, or donate to causes, but they don't necessarily see themselves as environmental leaders.

However, without a clear sense of purpose, it's hard to sustain environmental advocacy in the long term. It's easy to get discouraged by setbacks, overwhelmed by complexity, or distracted by other priorities. It's also easy to fall into the trap of doing what others expect you to do, rather than what you really care about.

This is where finding your why can make a difference. Your why is your intrinsic motivation for environmental advocacy. It's the reason behind your actions, the fuel for your passion, and the compass for your decisions. It's what gives you a sense of meaning, impact, and fulfillment in your environmental journey.

Finding your why is not a one-time event. It's a continuous process of self-discovery, reflection, and alignment. It requires you to explore your personal values, strengths, interests, and experiences. You must connect them to the broader environmental issues and opportunities. It also requires you to challenge your assumptions, biases, and limiting beliefs, and expand your horizons and possibilities.

Together, we will explore the importance of having a sense of purpose in environmental advocacy, the role of intrinsic motivation in sustaining action, and the challenge of aligning personal values with public issues. We will also provide strategies and exercises for finding your why, and examples of individuals who have found their why and made a difference in environmental advocacy.

2.1 IT'S NOT ENOUGH TO DO YOUR 9-5

If you're like most people, your job probably doesn't directly involve environmental advocacy or sustainability. You may work in a completely different field, such as finance, law, technology, or healthcare. You may feel like you don't have the time, resources, or expertise to make a significant impact on environmental issues outside of work.

However, relying on your 9-5 job alone to make a difference in the environment is often not enough. You may not fulfilled by your job, but you're too tired to do anything else. Join the club. Let's look at why making your passion for your environment a priority is key in developing leadership skills.

2.1.1   Limitations of conventional career paths

Most conventional careers, even those that are indirectly related to environmental issues, are designed to maximize profits or efficiency, rather than long-term sustainability or social and environmental justice. Even if you work for a company that claims to be environmentally responsible, its bottom line may still prioritize short-term financial gains over systemic change.

I work full time for an environmental nonprofit, and I find myself pretty drained by the end of my workday. I don't feel like I have enough energy to go out and do something else. Perhaps if you're like me, and already a leader in the environmental space, it will "be enough" - but many like me still do more.

A colleague of mine was just out doing a river clean up last weekend. Other colleagues lead hikes and kayaking trips. I make art in my off time, and very often, it has environmental themes laced throughout. Yes, we've all drunk the Kool-Aid of environmental justice, and it permeates through pretty much everything we do.

2.1.2   Volunteer activities complement and enhance

Even if your job provides some opportunities for environmental impact, you need to engage in extracurricular or volunteer activities to broaden your knowledge, skills, and connections in the environmental field. This can help you overcome the silos and biases of your professional network, and expose you to diverse perspectives, strategies, and challenges.

When we're out in the community, we're meeting new people and forming relationships. It's a chance for environmental evangelism, or in the very least, letting people know who you work for and why you love it. It can feel like a drag sometimes to take your one free day to go do other work, but it very often has benefits that show up through time.

2.1.3 Pursuing environmental advocacy as a personal passion and mission

Environmental advocacy can provide you with a sense of purpose, fulfillment, and identity that transcends your professional role or status. It can also help you develop transferable skills, such as leadership, communication, and resilience, that can enhance your professional performance and advancement. Additionally, pursuing environmental advocacy as a personal passion and mission can inspire and influence others around you. That means your family, friends, colleagues, and community.

When people know that you're an environmental leader, things start to fall into place. You may be asked to speak at a public hearing, or do an in-depth interview about that creek that really needs to be cleaned up behind your house. You might be able to get your city council or county government to actually listen. After all, you know people. *You could cause trouble for them.*

Environmental work is complementary to other types of social and justice work. I've fostered animals and worked closely with animal rescues for longer than I have been involved in the environmental movement. Many people have passions for vegetarianism, sustainable agriculture, and education that align closely with their environmental values. It's not a silo, and you're not required to stick to it. You're doing what makes you feel good - doing good - and that's great, wherever it takes you.

2.1.4 Looking beyond your day job

Therefore, it's important to look beyond your 9-5 job and explore other ways to make a difference in the environment. This can include volunteering for environmental organizations, participating in community events and campaigns, pursuing environmental education and certifications, starting your own environmental projects or businesses, or engaging in advocacy and policy-making at the local or national level.

By doing so, you can leverage your personal passion and mission for environmental advocacy, and complement and enhance your professional work with a broader perspective and purpose. You can also connect with a diverse and supportive network of environmental leaders, and contribute to a collective vision and action for a sustainable future.

2.2 FINDING WAYS TO SERVE YOUR COMMUNITY

Environmental advocacy is not just about global issues or distant ecosystems. It's also about the communities and neighborhoods where we live, work, and play. By engaging with our local community, we can make a tangible and meaningful impact on environmental health, equity, and resilience.

Here are some ways to serve your community and promote environmental advocacy:

2.2.1 Volunteering

There are numerous environmental organizations and initiatives that depend on volunteers to support their mission. You can volunteer for activities such as beach cleanups, tree plantings, habitat restorations, environmental education, or policy advocacy. Volunteering is a great way to meet like-minded people, learn new skills, and contribute to positive change in your community.

Volunteering for sustainability and environmental activities is easy, but sometimes, people don't know how to get started. Here are a few ideas to get your activities rolling.

1. Participate in (or organize) a local river or beach cleanup
2. Join a neighborhood garden club or community garden
3. Help to organize a community recycling program
4. Assist with wildlife rehabilitation efforts
5. Volunteer at a local nature center or park
6. Serve as a water quality monitor for your local streams and rivers
7. Organize an Earth Day (April 22) or Arbor Day (last Fri. in April) event in your community
8. Conduct energy audits or weatherization projects for low-income households
9. Advocate for public ecological education within the community
10. Help to start a composting initiative for the community

11. Work on public transit to improve accessibility and reduce carbon emissions

12. Advocate for sustainable infrastructure, including green buildings and renewable energy

13. Join or organize a community-led climate action group

14. Help to raise awareness about the effects of climate change through public forums or discussions

15. Assist with local conservation campaigns

16. Participate in tree-planting events or reforestation projects

17. Educate residents about ways to reduce waste and pollution in their homes

18. Participate in citizen science projects that track biodiversity or air quality

19. Work with local schools to promote environmental education and sustainability

20. Advocate for a local clean energy transition plan

21. Join or create a community-supported agriculture program

22. Support local farmers' markets and buy locally grown produce

23. Work on a community garden or urban farm

24. Help to organize a plastic bag reduction campaign

25. Participate in campaigns for wildlife protection and habitat restoration

> These are just a few examples of the many ways that you can volunteer in your community as an environmental advocate. You can also reach out to local environmental organizations, community centers, or government agencies to find out about other opportunities that fit your skills and interests. Remember that every small action counts, and that community engagement is essential for building a sustainable and equitable future.

Nonprofits especially love volunteers with specialist skills. If you're a lawyer, designer, or finance professional, nonprofits will literally beg you to volunteer. Most likely as a board member. Decide ahead of time - before you're asked - whether you're interested in a position on a nonprofit board, as it can be quite time consuming. Even if you pass on the board, chances are you can still serve a local nonprofit with your skills.

2.2.2 Activism

If you're passionate about a particular environmental issue or cause, you can join or create a local activist group. Activism can take many forms, such as protests, rallies, petitions, letter-writing campaigns, or civil disobedience. Activism requires courage, persistence, and collaboration, but it can also generate attention, momentum, and impact on environmental policy and public opinion.

1. Sign and share online petitions related to environmental issues

2. Attend town hall meetings or city council meetings to voice your concerns on environmental matters

3. Participate in peaceful demonstrations for environmental causes

4. Write letters to elected officials advocating for environmental policies

5. Attend public hearings on environmental issues

6. Share news articles and research studies related to environmental issues on social media

7. Join local environmental organizations and attend their events and meetings

8. Start a letter-writing campaign to local newspapers or elected officials

9. Participate in an environmental lobby day at the state or national level

10. Contact companies and corporations about their environmental practices

11. Join or start a community group to reduce waste and promote recycling

12. Attend workshops and conferences related to environmental activism and sustainability

13. Participate in boycotts of companies that have poor environmental records

14. Start an environmental club at your school or workplace

15. Create and distribute educational materials about the environment

16. Host a film screening or educational event about environmental issues

17. Organize a community garden or urban farm

18. Work with local schools to promote environmental education and sustainability

19. Host clean-up events in green spaces or along waterways

20. Advocate for protected areas and wildlife conservation

21. Support and donate to environmental campaigns and initiatives

22. Write op-eds for local newspapers or online platforms

23. Create and share educational videos or infographics on environmental issues

24. Host educational booths at community events to raise awareness about environmental issues

25. Participate in citizen science projects to collect data on environmental health

These are just a few examples of the many ways that you can get involved in environmental activism efforts. Remember that every action counts, no matter how small, in creating a more sustainable and equitable world.

2.2.3 Entrepreneurship

If you have an innovative idea or solution for an environmental challenge, you can start your own environmental business or social enterprise. Entrepreneurship can provide you with autonomy, creativity, and scalability in pursuing your environmental vision. It can also create jobs, wealth, and community benefits, while reducing environmental harm.

Entrepreneurship is not an overnight thing, but if you're interested in running your own environmentally themed business, here are some ideas.

1. Eco-friendly cleaning service using non-toxic and sustainable products
2. Organic produce delivery service
3. Sustainable fashion brand using environmentally-friendly materials
4. Upcycling or repurposing business
5. Zero-waste grocery store
6. Composting service for households or businesses
7. Green energy consulting service
8. Electric vehicle charging station installation and maintenance services
9. Organic food truck or restaurant
10. Eco-friendly landscaping services
11. Reusable water bottle or food container brand

12. Bike rental or sharing business

13. Rainwater harvesting system installation and maintenance services

14. Sustainable architecture and design firm

15. Solar panel installation and maintenance services

16. Sustainable event planning and coordination services

17. Brand consulting for environmentally-focused nonprofits or socially-responsible businesses

18. Sustainable furniture or home décor manufacturing

19. Bicycle courier or delivery service

20. Green transportation company using electric or hybrid vehicles

21. Environmental education and training services

22. Community compost program creation and management

23. Waste reduction consulting services for businesses

24. Organic beauty and personal care product line

25. Environmental research and development company

These are just a few examples of the many ways that you can start a business while promoting environmental advocacy. Remember that entrepreneurship can provide unique opportunities for innovation, collaboration, and impact on environmental sustainability and social justice.

2.2.4 Considerations for Choosing the Right Type of Activity

When choosing the right type of service that fits your skills, interests, and context, it's important to consider factors such as your availability, resources, and goals. You may want to assess your strengths and weaknesses, your network and affiliations, your learning and growth opportunities, and your potential impact and outcomes. You may also want to seek advice or feedback from others who have experience in the field.

By serving your community in these ways, you can not only promote environmental advocacy but also learn more about the challenges and opportunities of local sustainability. You can also raise awareness and inspire others to take action, and build relationships and networks that can support your future environmental leadership.

2.2.5 Stepping up to the plate

Environmental leadership is not just about holding a position of authority or expertise. It's also about taking initiative and responsibility for environmental issues, even when it's difficult or unpopular. Proactive environmental leaders have a mindset and behavior that prioritize long-term sustainability and social and environmental justice over short-term profits or convenience.

Here are some examples of individuals who have made a significant difference through their actions:

- Wangari Maathai, who founded the Green Belt Movement in Kenya and planted over 50 million trees to empower women, restore degraded land, and promote democracy

- Greta Thunberg, who initiated the school strike for climate movement and inspired millions of young people to demand urgent action on climate change from politicians and businesses

- Bill McKibben, who co-founded 350.org and launched the fossil fuel divestment campaign to challenge the power and influence of the fossil fuel industry and accelerate the transition to renewable energy

- Vandana Shiva, who founded Navdanya and promotes agro-ecological farming and seed-saving to preserve biodiversity, food sovereignty, and cultural heritage

These individuals demonstrate the courage, vision, and impact of proactive environmental leadership. They also face many challenges and opportunities in their journey, such as:

- Resistance and opposition from powerful stakeholders who benefit from the status quo
- Lack of resources, support, or recognition from mainstream institutions or society
- Emotional and physical exhaustion from working in high-stress and high-risk environments
- The potential for burnout, disillusionment, or cynicism from setbacks or failures
- The need for collaboration, learning, and self-reflection to sustain and improve their leadership practice

You don't need to go to jail to be an environmental leader. There are environmental leaders everywhere, you only need to open a newspaper (online, of course), or visit a local meeting to start identifying them. And you, too, may already be seen as an environmental leader in your day-to-day activities.

Stepping up to the plate in environmental leadership requires not only a strong passion and commitment but also a realistic and adaptable approach. It requires continuous learning, creativity, and collaboration. It also requires a recognition of one's own privilege, bias, and limitations. You must be willing to listen, learn, and empower those who are most affected by environmental issues.

By embracing proactive environmental leadership, we can make a positive and lasting impact on the environment and society. We can inspire and mobilize others to join us, and create a more sustainable and just world for all.

2.3 STRATEGIES FOR FINDING YOUR WHY

Environmental advocacy can be a challenging and complex endeavor that requires a strong sense of purpose and motivation. To sustain and enhance your environmental leadership, it's important to identify and articulate your personal why for environmental advocacy. Your why is the underlying reason or value that drives and guides your environmental actions and decisions.

Here are some strategies for finding your why:

2.3.1 Self-reflection

By taking time to reflect on your values, experiences, and aspirations, you can gain clarity and insight into your personal why. You can use techniques such as journaling, mindfulness, or coaching to explore your thoughts and feelings related to environmental issues and their connection to your life purpose.

2.3.1.1 Life Story

Write a brief autobiography of your life, focusing on the pivotal moments, people, and experiences that have shaped your values, beliefs, and interests. Look for patterns or themes that relate to environmental issues or solutions. Reflect on how your life story informs your why for environmental advocacy.

2.3.1.2   Visioning Exercise

Imagine yourself in the future, ten years from now. Visualize a world where environmental sustainability is the norm, and where everyone acts responsibly and collaboratively to protect the planet. Describe what this world looks like, feels like, and sounds like. Reflect on how this vision aligns with your why for environmental advocacy, and what steps you can take to make it a reality.

2.3.2   Sources of inspiration and role models

By learning from others who have demonstrated passion, commitment, and impact in environmental advocacy, you can find inspiration and guidance on how to discover and pursue your own why. You can read biographies, interviews, or speeches of environmental leaders, attend their events or webinars, or join their networks or communities.

Identify one or more environmental leaders or activists whom you admire or respect. Research their life stories, values, strategies, and impact. Reflect on what inspires you about them, and how you can apply their lessons or insights to your own why for environmental advocacy.

2.3.3   Values Clarification

Make a list of your top five personal values (e.g., honesty, creativity, compassion, learning, freedom). For each value, write down how it relates to environmental advocacy. Then, prioritize them according to their importance to you. Reflect on how your values inform your why for environmental advocacy.

2.3.4 Impact Map

Draw a map of the environmental issues or causes that you care about. For each issue, identify the stakeholders who are affected by it (e.g., communities, ecosystems, species, industries, governments), and the actions that can be taken to address it (e.g., policy changes, behavior changes, innovation, education). Reflect on which issues resonate most with your why for environmental advocacy.

2.3.5 Filtering out the fluff

Finally, finding your why is important for understanding which projects and activities you should take on - and which ones you should pass on. If I'm tight on time, that means I should be taking on projects that are most closely aligned with my personal values. If I don't know my why, that may be a struggle.

For me, my why is to leave the world better than I found it. And my how is by building up the next generation of environmental leaders. Under that umbrella, I'm more likely to take a teaching opportunity than build houses for Habitat for Humanity - although I do love home construction. Knowing your why - and ultimately, your "how" - is critical for understanding how you'll move in this world.

2.4 CONCLUSION

In this chapter, we explored strategies for finding your personal why for environmental advocacy. We learned that identifying and articulating your why can provide clarity, motivation, and alignment for your environmental actions and decisions.

2.4.1 Key Takeaways

- Self-reflection and introspection can help you understand your values, interests, and aspirations related to the environment.

- Learning from inspiring role models and communities can provide guidance and inspiration for your environmental leadership.

- Structured exercises can help you clarify and articulate your personal why for environmental advocacy.

- It's not enough to do your 9-5. You must do other activities to stay refreshed and connected, within and around the environmental world.

- Finding ways to serve your community. Finding activities in a small town can be challenging. We provide some ideas for changing the world right in your backyard.

- Stepping up to the plate. Being a leader isn't something that happens TO you. It's something that you CHOOSE to do.

- Strategies for finding your why. Froom journaling to experimenting, there are many ways that you can find out what it is you care about.

  The potential impact of finding your why for environmental advocacy is significant. By aligning your personal and environmental values and goals, you can activate your intrinsic motivation, overcome challenges and setbacks, and sustain your environmental leadership in the long term. You can also inspire and connect with others who share your vision and values, and create a collective impact that benefits both people and the planet.

I invite you to try out the strategies for finding your why and share your insights with others. By engaging in ongoing learning and reflection, and by collaborating and communicating with others, we can create a more sustainable and just world for everyone. Remember that every action counts, and that by taking responsibility for our environmental impact, we can make a positive difference in the world.

What motivates you to care about the environment? What drives you to take action, make sacrifices, and overcome obstacles for the sake of nature? What is your why for environmental advocacy?

2.4.2 Reflection Questions

1. How have you gone beyond your 9-5 job to engage in environmental advocacy or sustainability? What motivated you to do so, and what challenges have you faced?

2. What are some ways you can serve your community or neighborhood to promote environmental health and equity? How can you involve others in these activities and generate positive impact?

3. What does it mean to "step up to the plate" in environmental leadership? What are some examples of individuals who have done so, and what lessons can you learn from them?

4. Which strategies for finding your why resonated with you the most? Have you tried any of them before? What insights or discoveries did you gain from them, and how did they inform your environmental advocacy?

5. How do you balance your personal passion and mission for environmental advocacy with your professional responsibilities and priorities? What are some ways you can align them and leverage their synergy for better outcomes?

6.   What is your vision for becoming an environmental leader?
     What impact do you want to make, and how do you plan to
     achieve it? Who are your allies and collaborators in this
     journey, and how can you support each other?

7.   What scares you in the community, neighborhood,
     government, or environmental issues that you care about?
     What steps can you take to conquer those fears today?

3 Understanding Environmental Leadership

Leadership is essential in shaping our world, and environmental leadership has become increasingly vital in today's society. Environmental leaders are individuals who use their skills, knowledge, and passion to address environmental challenges and promote sustainability. Environmental leadership can take many forms, from grassroots activism to corporate responsibility to public policy advocacy.

In this chapter, we will provide an overview of environmental leadership, including its definition, importance, and qualities of a good, sane, and equitable environmental leader.

3.1 Defining Environmental Leadership

Environmental leadership involves taking action to address environmental issues and promoting sustainable practices. It requires a commitment to environmental stewardship, social justice, and community engagement. Environmental leaders may come from various sectors, such as government, business, civil society, or academia, and may have different backgrounds and experiences.

3.1.1 Importance of Environmental Leadership in Today's Society

Environmental leadership is critical in addressing urgent global challenges, such as climate change, biodiversity loss, or pollution. It can help create a more sustainable, equitable, and resilient world by fostering innovation, collaboration, and social and environmental justice. Environmental leadership can also inspire and mobilize others to take action and create positive change.

3.1.2   Understanding the Qualities of a Good, Sane, and Equitable
Environmental Leader

What makes an effective environmental leader? While there is no one-size-fits-all answer, some qualities that are often associated with successful environmental leadership include:

- Vision: Having a clear and inspiring vision of a sustainable and just future
- Courage: Being willing to take risks, face opposition, and speak truth to power
- Collaboration: Building partnerships and coalitions across sectors and disciplines
- Empathy: Understanding and respecting the perspectives and needs of diverse stakeholders
- Adaptability: Being flexible, agile, and able to learn from failures and feedback
- Ethics: Upholding ethical principles and values, such as honesty, transparency, and accountability
- Inclusivity: Promoting diversity, equity, and inclusion in decision-making and outcomes

By cultivating these qualities, environmental leaders can become effective change agents and role models for others.

In conclusion, environmental leadership is a vital component of a sustainable and just world. It requires a commitment to environmental stewardship, social justice, and community engagement. Understanding the qualities of a good, sane, and equitable environmental leader is essential to cultivate effective environmental leadership skills. In the following sections, we will explore different models and frameworks of environmental leadership, core competencies and qualities of effective environmental leaders, and case studies of exceptional environmental leaders.

3.2 IMPORTANCE OF ENVIRONMENTAL LEADERSHIP

Environmental leadership plays a crucial role in addressing environmental challenges and promoting sustainable development. In this section, we will explore the various ways in which environmental leadership impacts public policy and decision-making, sustainable development, and social justice.

The Role of Environmental Leadership in Shaping Public Policy and Decision-Making

Environmental leaders can play a significant role in shaping public policy and decision-making on environmental issues. By advocating for evidence-based policies and practices, mobilizing public opinion, and engaging with stakeholders, environmental leaders can influence the direction and effectiveness of environmental regulations and programs.

For example, environmental leaders have been instrumental in advancing climate change legislation, such as the Paris Agreement, and promoting renewable energy and energy efficiency policies. They have also worked to hold businesses and governments accountable for their environmental impact, through campaigns such as divestment from fossil fuels and corporate responsibility initiatives.

3.2.1 The Impact of Environmental Leadership on Sustainable Development

Environmental leadership is essential in promoting sustainable development, which aims to meet the needs of the present without compromising the ability of future generations to meet their own needs. By advocating for sustainable practices and policies, environmental leaders can help ensure the long-term viability of natural resources, ecosystems, and human communities.

For instance, environmental leaders have played a key role in promoting sustainable agriculture, conservation of biodiversity, and reduction of waste and pollution. They have also contributed to the development of sustainable urban and transportation systems, green infrastructure, and eco-tourism.

3.2.2 The Link Between Environmental Leadership and Social Justice

Environmental leadership is closely linked to social justice, which seeks to ensure equitable access to resources, opportunities, and benefits for all members of society, regardless of their ethnicity, gender, income, or other factors. Environmental issues often disproportionately affect marginalized communities, such as low-income households, indigenous peoples, or people of color. By addressing these inequities, environmental leaders can promote a more just and equitable world.

For example, environmental leaders have advocated for the rights of indigenous peoples to protect their lands and cultures from environmental degradation and extractive industries. They have also worked to reduce environmental health disparities, such as exposure to air and water pollution, in low-income communities and communities of color.

In conclusion, environmental leadership is essential in shaping public policy and decision-making, promoting sustainable development, and advancing social justice. By engaging in environmental leadership, individuals can make a positive impact on society and the environment, and inspire others to do the same.

3.2.3 Identifying Environmental Leaders: The SPEND Framework

Environmental leadership takes many forms and can come from a variety of sectors and contexts. Here are some different models and frameworks of environmental leadership. In brief: - **Superheroes** - Superheroes are people who believe relentlessly in righting environmental injustices, even when the odds seem stacked against them. They see environmental problems as social justice issues and use their determination and courage to fight for change. - **Politicians** - Politicians are people who use their political power and influence to advance environmental goals. They are often willing to make deals and compromise to achieve their objectives. - **Earth Stewards** - Earth stewards are people who are driven by a moral or religious obligation to care for the earth and its creatures. They see environmental stewardship as a personal and spiritual responsibility and often emphasize the interconnectedness of all living things. - **Nerds** - Nerds are people who are obsessed with an issue and need to find the answer. They use their deep expertise and knowledge to understand complex environmental problems and develop innovative solutions. - **Disruptors** - Disruptors are people who challenge the status quo and make waves to bring attention to environmental issues. They may use tactics such as civil disobedience, protests, and media campaigns to draw attention to environmental problems and push for change.

3.3 SUPERHEROES

Superheroes are people who believe relentlessly in righting environmental injustices, even when the odds seem stacked against them. They see environmental problems as social justice issues and use their determination and courage to fight for change. Superheroes can be effective in challenging systemic inequalities and promoting equity and justice in environmental decision-making. Examples of environmental superheroes include Erin Brockovich, the consumer advocate and environmental activist who fought against corporate pollution, and Lois Gibbs, the founder of the Love Canal Homeowners Association and environmental justice pioneer.

Overall, environmental leadership takes many forms and can come from a variety of sectors and contexts. By understanding the different models and frameworks of environmental leadership, we can identify and support a diverse range of environmental leaders who can make a positive impact on the environment and society.

3.3.1 Erin Brockovich

Erin Brockovich is an American environmental activist and consumer advocate who rose to national prominence for her role in exposing a major groundwater contamination case in Hinkley, California. She is a prime example of a "superhero" environmental leader - someone who believes relentlessly in righting environmental injustices, even when the odds seem stacked against them.

1. **Courageous Advocacy:** Erin Brockovich is known for her courageous advocacy on behalf of communities affected by environmental contamination. Her work in Hinkley, California,

helped to expose a major environmental injustice and led to a $333 million settlement for the affected residents. She has continued to advocate for environmental justice and consumer protection throughout her career.

2. **Relentless Determination:** Brockovich's relentless determination has made her a powerful force for change. She never gives up on fighting for environmental justice, even in the face of formidable opposition. Her persistence has led to numerous victories for affected communities and has inspired others to take action.

3. **Seeing Environmental Problems as Social Justice Issues:** Brockovich sees environmental problems as social justice issues and recognizes that vulnerable communities are disproportionately affected by environmental hazards. She advocates for policies that prioritize the health and well-being of all communities, regardless of their socio-economic status.

4. **Empowering Communities:** Brockovich empowers communities to take action and make a difference. She works to educate and mobilize affected communities to demand change and hold polluters accountable. Her work has inspired numerous grassroots movements for environmental justice and consumer protection.

5. **Inspiring Others:** Erin Brockovich's leadership and advocacy have inspired countless individuals to take action towards environmental justice and consumer protection. Her story has been told in books, movies, and television shows, and she has become a symbol of hope for those seeking to make a difference in the face of environmental challenges.

In conclusion, Erin Brockovich is an excellent example of a "superhero" environmental leader who believes relentlessly in righting environmental injustices. Her courageous advocacy, relentless determination, and commitment to seeing environmental problems as social justice issues have made her a powerful force for change. She inspires others to take action and make a difference in the fight for environmental justice and consumer protection.

3.3.2   Lois Gibbs

Lois Gibbs is an American environmental activist who rose to prominence for her efforts to expose and remediate environmental contamination in the Love Canal neighborhood of Niagara Falls, New York. She is a prime example of a "superhero" environmental leader - someone who believes relentlessly in righting environmental injustices, even when the odds seem stacked against them.

1.   **Courageous Advocacy:** Lois Gibbs is known for her courageous advocacy on behalf of communities affected by environmental contamination. She mobilized her community to demand action when she discovered that their homes were built on top of a toxic waste dump. Her advocacy led to the relocation of over 800 families and the creation of the Superfund program, which provides funding for the cleanup of hazardous waste sites.

2.   **Relentless Determination:** Gibbs' relentless determination has made her a powerful force for change. Despite facing numerous obstacles, including harassment and intimidation, she never gave up on fighting for environmental justice. Her persistence has led to numerous victories for affected communities and has inspired others to take action.

3. **Seeing Environmental Problems as Social Justice Issues:**
    Gibbs sees environmental problems as social justice issues and
    recognizes that vulnerable communities are
    disproportionately affected by environmental hazards. She
    advocates for policies that prioritize the health and well-being
    of all communities, regardless of their socio-economic status.

4. **Empowering Communities:** Gibbs empowers communities to
    take action and make a difference. She works to educate and
    mobilize affected communities to demand change and hold
    polluters accountable. Her work has inspired numerous
    grassroots movements for environmental justice.

5. **Inspiring Others:** Lois Gibbs' leadership and advocacy have
    inspired countless individuals to take action towards
    environmental justice. Her story has been told in books,
    movies, and television shows, and she has become a symbol of
    hope for those seeking to make a difference in the face of
    environmental challenges.

    In conclusion, Lois Gibbs is an excellent example of a
    "superhero" environmental leader who believes
    relentlessly in righting environmental injustices. Her
    courageous advocacy, relentless determination, and
    commitment to seeing environmental problems as social
    justice issues have made her a powerful force for change.
    She inspires others to take action and make a difference
    in the fight for environmental justice.

3.4 POLITICIANS

Politicians are people who use their political power and influence to advance environmental goals. They are often willing to make deals and compromise to achieve their objectives. Political leaders can be effective in implementing policies and programs that promote sustainable development and address environmental problems. Examples of political environmental leaders include Al Gore, the former Vice President of the United States and advocate for climate action, and Marina Silva, the former Minister of Environment in Brazil who helped reduce deforestation in the Amazon.

3.4.1 Marina Silva

Marina Silva is a Brazilian politician and environmental leader who has dedicated her career to promoting sustainable development and protecting the Amazon rainforest. As Brazil's former Minister of Environment, she implemented innovative policies and initiatives that helped reduce deforestation and promote conservation. Here are some of the reasons why Marina Silva is an excellent example of a politician-style environmental leader:

1. **Commitment to Environmental Protection:** Marina Silva has demonstrated a deep commitment to environmental protection and sustainability throughout her career. She grew up in poverty in the Amazon and experienced firsthand the devastating impacts of deforestation and pollution on local communities and ecosystems. Her personal experiences motivated her to become an environmental advocate and work to protect the Amazon and its people.

2. **Political Savvy:** As a politician, Marina Silva is skilled in navigating complex political landscapes and building support

for environmental policies and programs. She has worked with multiple administrations and parties in Brazil and has been able to promote environmental initiatives even during times of economic or political instability.

3. **Innovative Policies:** Marina Silva developed and implemented innovative policies and initiatives as Brazil's Minister of Environment from 2003 to 2008. During this time, she helped establish protected areas in the Amazon, implemented a program to pay small-scale farmers to protect forests, and encouraged private sector engagement in sustainable development. These policies helped reduce deforestation and promote conservation in Brazil.

4. **International Recognition:** Marina Silva's environmental leadership has been recognized internationally. In 2007, she was awarded the United Nations Champions of the Earth award for her work to protect the environment. She has also been recognized by TIME magazine as one of the world's most influential people and by Forbes as one of the world's most powerful women.

5. **Grassroots Support:** Marina Silva has strong grassroots support from environmental organizations, indigenous communities, and social movements. She is known for her ability to mobilize public opinion and build coalitions to advance environmental causes.

> Marina Silva is an excellent example of a politician-style environmental leader who has made significant contributions to sustainable development and conservation in Brazil and beyond. Her commitment to environmental protection, political savvy, innovative policies, international recognition, and grassroots support demonstrate the core competencies and qualities of effective environmental leadership. Her leadership serves as an inspiration to others who seek to promote sustainable development and protect the environment.

3.4.2 Alexandria Ocasio-Cortez

Alexandria Ocasio-Cortez, also known as AOC, is a United States congresswoman and environmental leader who has made significant contributions to the fight against climate change in the United States. She is a vocal advocate for bold action on climate change, and her Green New Deal proposal has become a rallying cry for environmental activists across the country. Here are some of the reasons why AOC is an excellent example of a politician-style environmental leader:

1. **Bold Vision:** AOC has articulated a bold vision for a sustainable future through her Green New Deal proposal. The plan sets ambitious goals for reducing greenhouse gas emissions, transitioning to renewable energy, creating green jobs, and promoting social justice. Her vision has inspired a new generation of environmental activists and has helped shift the conversation on climate change in the United States.

2. **Political Savvy:** As a congresswoman, AOC has shown political savvy in advocating for environmental policies and programs. She has built alliances with other progressive lawmakers, mobilized public opinion through social media and grassroots organizing, and taken on powerful fossil fuel interests in Congress and beyond.

3. **Passionate Advocacy:** AOC is a passionate advocate for environmental causes and has used her platform as a congresswoman to speak out on the urgency of the climate crisis. She has participated in protests and direct actions to raise awareness of environmental issues and has given impassioned speeches on the House floor calling for action on climate change.

4. **Grassroots Support:** AOC has strong grassroots support from environmental organizations, youth groups, and progressive

activists. She has been able to mobilize public opinion and build coalitions to advance environmental causes and push for policy change.

5. **Intersectional Approach:** AOC has taken an intersectional approach to environmental leadership, recognizing the connections between social justice and environmental issues. She has emphasized the need to address systemic inequalities in the transition to a sustainable economy and has advocated for policies that promote equity and justice.

Alexandria Ocasio-Cortez is an excellent example of a politician-style environmental leader who has made significant contributions to the fight against climate change in the United States. Her bold vision, political savvy, passionate advocacy, grassroots support, and intersectional approach demonstrate the core competencies and qualities of effective environmental leadership. Her leadership serves as an inspiration to others who seek to promote sustainability and environmental justice in their communities and beyond.

3.5   EARTH STEWARDS

Earth stewards are people who are driven by a moral or religious obligation to care for the earth and its creatures. They see environmental stewardship as a personal and spiritual responsibility and often emphasize the interconnectedness of all living things.

Earth stewards can be effective in promoting sustainable lifestyles and values and inspiring others to take action on environmental issues. Examples of environmental stewards include Reverend Leo Woodberry, the environmental justice leader and founder of the Kingdom Living Temple, and Father John Rausch, the Catholic priest and Appalachian environmental advocate.

3.5.1 Reverend Leo Woodberry

Reverend Leo Woodberry is an American environmental activist and founder of the New Alpha Community Development Corporation. He is a prime example of an "earth steward" environmental leader - someone who is driven by a moral or religious obligation to care for the earth and its creatures.

1. **Moral and Religious Obligation:** Reverend Leo Woodberry's passion for environmental stewardship is grounded in his faith. He sees environmental stewardship as a personal and spiritual responsibility and is driven by a sense of moral obligation to care for the earth and its creatures. He believes that taking care of the earth is an essential part of his faith and encourages others to see it in the same way.

2. **Interconnectedness of All Living Things:** Woodberry emphasizes the interconnectedness of all living things. He recognizes that environmental degradation affects not only the earth but also humans and other creatures. He advocates for policies that prioritize the health and well-being of all living things, not just humans.

3. **Community Empowerment:** Woodberry works to empower communities to take action towards environmental stewardship. He founded the New Alpha Community Development Corporation to promote sustainable development and renewable energy in low-income and marginalized communities. He believes that everyone has a role to play in environmental stewardship and works to ensure that everyone has the resources and knowledge they need to make a difference.

4. **Advocacy for Policy Change:** Woodberry's deep commitment to environmental stewardship has made him a vocal advocate for policy change. He has spoken before Congress and worked

with policymakers to promote policies that prioritize environmental stewardship and sustainability.

5. **Inspiring Others:** Reverend Leo Woodberry's leadership and advocacy have inspired countless individuals to take action towards environmental stewardship. His emphasis on the moral and religious obligation to care for the earth and its creatures resonates with many people and has motivated them to see environmental stewardship as a personal and spiritual responsibility.

In conclusion, Reverend Leo Woodberry is an excellent example of an "earth steward" environmental leader who is driven by a moral or religious obligation to care for the earth and its creatures. His emphasis on the interconnectedness of all living things, community empowerment, advocacy for policy change, and inspiration of others make him a powerful force for environmental stewardship and sustainability.

3.5.2   Father John Rausch

Father John Rausch is an American Catholic priest and environmental activist who has dedicated his life to promoting sustainable development and environmental justice. He is a prime example of an "earth steward" environmental leader - someone who is driven by a moral or religious obligation to care for the earth and its creatures.

1. **Moral and Religious Obligation:** Father John Rausch's passion for environmental stewardship is grounded in his faith. He sees environmental stewardship as a personal and spiritual responsibility and is driven by a sense of moral obligation to care for the earth and its creatures. He believes that taking care of the earth is an essential part of his faith and encourages others to see it in the same way.

2. **Interconnectedness of All Living Things:** Rausch emphasizes the interconnectedness of all living things. He recognizes that environmental degradation affects not only the earth but also humans and other creatures. He advocates for policies that prioritize the health and well-being of all living things, not just humans.

3. **Community Empowerment:** Rausch works to empower communities to take action towards environmental stewardship. He has helped to establish numerous community-based organizations focused on sustainable development and environmental justice. He believes that everyone has a role to play in environmental stewardship and works to ensure that everyone has the resources and knowledge they need to make a difference.

4. **Advocacy for Policy Change:** Rausch's commitment to environmental stewardship has made him a vocal advocate for policy change. He has spoken before Congress and worked with policymakers to promote policies that prioritize environmental stewardship and sustainability. He has also collaborated with other faith-based organizations to advance environmental justice.

5. **Inspiring Others:** Father John Rausch's leadership and advocacy have inspired countless individuals to take action towards environmental stewardship. His emphasis on the moral and religious obligation to care for the earth and its creatures resonates with many people and has motivated them to see environmental stewardship as a personal and spiritual responsibility.

In conclusion, Father John Rausch is an excellent example of an "earth steward" environmental leader who is driven by a moral or religious obligation to care for the earth and its creatures. His emphasis on the interconnectedness of all living things, community empowerment, advocacy for policy change, and inspiration of others make him a powerful force for environmental stewardship and sustainability. His work serves as an inspiration to all those who seek to promote environmental justice and sustainable development.

3.6 NERDS

Nerds are people who are obsessed with an issue and need to find the answer. They use their deep expertise and knowledge to understand complex environmental problems and develop innovative solutions. Nerds can be effective in developing new technologies and advancing scientific understanding of environmental challenges. Examples of environmental nerds include Bill Moomaw, the climate scientist who was the founding director of the Tufts Institute of the Environment, and Robert D. Bullard, the scholar of environmental justice who is known as the "father" of the environmental justice movement.

3.6.1 Bill Moomaw

Bill Moomaw is an American environmental scientist and professor who has dedicated his career to researching and promoting sustainable development. He is a prime example of a "nerd" environmental leader - someone who is deeply passionate about the details of environmental science and policy and uses this knowledge to drive action towards sustainability.

1. **Passion for Environmental Research:** Bill Moomaw has a deep passion for environmental research and understanding

complex environmental issues. He has spent his career conducting research in fields such as climate change, renewable energy, and sustainable development. He has published over fifty papers and reports on these topics, demonstrating his commitment to understanding the nuances of environmental challenges.

2. **Innovative Solutions:** Moomaw is known for his innovative solutions to environmental problems. He has proposed a range of solutions to reduce greenhouse gas emissions, including proforestation (allowing forests to mature) as a large scale carbon capture strategy, and the transition to truly clean renewable energy sources such as wind and solar power.

3. **Attention to Detail:** As a "nerd" environmental leader, Moomaw is well-known for his attention to detail and his focus on finding answers to complex environmental questions. He is constantly seeking new information and insights to deepen his understanding of environmental challenges and develop effective solutions.

4. **Advocacy for Policy Change:** Moomaw's expertise in environmental science and policy has made him a vocal advocate for policy change. He has advised governments, non-profit organizations, and businesses on sustainable development issues and has worked to influence policy outcomes at local, national, and international levels.

5. **Impactful Contributions:** Moomaw's contributions to environmental science and policy have been impactful and influential. He was a lead author for five major Intergovernmental Panel on Climate Change Reports. His work has informed policy decisions and shaped public opinion on environmental issues.

In conclusion, Bill Moomaw is an excellent example of a "nerd" environmental leader who is passionate about the details of environmental science and policy. He uses his knowledge to develop innovative solutions to environmental challenges and advocates for policy change at all levels. His contributions to environmental science and policy have been impactful and influential and serve as an inspiration to all those who are dedicated to advancing sustainability and protecting the environment.

3.6.2 Robert D. Bullard

Robert D. Bullard is a leading environmental justice scholar and activist who has dedicated his career to researching and advocating for the equitable distribution of environmental benefits and burdens. He is a prime example of a "nerd" environmental leader - someone who is deeply passionate about the details of environmental justice and uses this knowledge to drive action towards equity.

1. **Pioneering Environmental Justice Research:** Robert D. Bullard is widely regarded as the "father of environmental justice." He has spent over four decades conducting research on the disproportionate impacts of environmental hazards on low-income communities and communities of color. His work has helped to shed light on the systemic causes of environmental injustice and has driven policy change at all levels of government.

2. **Attention to Detail:** As a "nerd" environmental leader, Bullard is known for his attention to detail and his focus on finding answers to complex environmental justice questions. He has developed innovative methodologies for analyzing the distribution of environmental hazards and identifying patterns of environmental discrimination.

3. **Intersectional Approach:** Bullard has been a vocal advocate for an intersectional approach to environmental justice. He recognizes that environmental injustices are intertwined with social and economic inequalities and advocates for policies that address these interconnections.

4. **Advocacy for Policy Change:** Bullard's expertise in environmental justice has made him a powerful advocate for policy change. He has advised governments, non-profit organizations, and grassroots activists on strategies for advancing environmental justice and has testified before Congress on multiple occasions.

5. **Impactful Contributions:** Bullard's contributions to environmental justice research and advocacy have been impactful and transformative. His work has informed policy decisions and shaped public opinion on environmental justice issues. He has received numerous awards and accolades for his contributions to the field of environmental justice.

In conclusion, Robert D. Bullard is an excellent example of a "nerd" environmental leader who is passionate about the details of environmental justice. He uses his knowledge to develop innovative solutions to environmental injustices and advocates for policy change at all levels. His contributions to environmental justice research and advocacy have been impactful and transformative, and serve as an inspiration to all those who are dedicated to advancing equity and justice in the environmental arena.

3.7 DISRUPTORS

Disruptors are people who challenge the status quo and make waves to bring attention to environmental issues. They may use tactics such as civil disobedience, protests, and media campaigns to draw attention to environmental problems and push for change. Disruptors can be effective in raising public awareness and mobilizing support for environmental causes. Examples of environmental disruptors include Greta Thunberg, the teenage climate activist who has inspired global youth climate strikes, and Wangari Maathai, the Kenyan environmentalist who founded the Green Belt Movement to promote reforestation and women's rights.

3.7.1 Greta Thunberg

Greta Thunberg is a Swedish environmental activist who has become a global icon for her leadership in the fight against climate change. She is a vocal advocate for urgent action on climate change and has used disruptive tactics to raise awareness of environmental issues and push for policy change. Here are some of the reasons why Greta Thunberg is an excellent example of a disruptor-style environmental leader:

1. **Bold Action:** Greta Thunberg has taken bold action to raise awareness of environmental issues and push for policy change. She has inspired youth climate strikes around the world and has confronted world leaders at international summits to demand action on climate change.

2. **Media Savvy:** Greta Thunberg has been media savvy in leveraging social media and mainstream news outlets to spread her message and build a global movement. She has used Twitter, Instagram, and other platforms to connect with followers and share updates on her activism.

3. **Youth Leadership:** Greta Thunberg has emerged as a powerful leader of the youth climate movement, inspiring a new generation of environmental activists to take action on climate change. She has emphasized the importance of youth leadership and has called on young people around the world to demand action from their governments and institutions.

4. **Direct Action:** Greta Thunberg has used direct action tactics such as strikes, protests, and civil disobedience to draw attention to environmental issues and push for policy change. She has refused to fly to reduce her carbon footprint and has sailed across the Atlantic Ocean to attend international climate summits.

5. **Moral Clarity:** Greta Thunberg has demonstrated moral clarity in articulating the urgency of the climate crisis and calling for immediate action. She has challenged world leaders to listen to the science and take bold steps to reduce greenhouse gas emissions and protect the planet.

    Greta Thunberg is an excellent example of a disruptor-style environmental leader who has made significant contributions to the fight against climate change. Her bold action, media savvy, youth leadership, direct action, and moral clarity demonstrate the core competencies and qualities of effective environmental leadership. Her leadership serves as an inspiration to others who seek to disrupt the status quo and drive change on environmental issues.

3.7.2   Wangari Maathai

Wangari Maathai was a Kenyan environmentalist and activist who was the first African woman to receive the Nobel Peace Prize in 2004. She was a visionary leader who recognized the interconnectedness of social justice and environmental preservation. Maathai founded the Green Belt Movement, which empowered women to plant trees and restore degraded land in Kenya. Here are some of the reasons why Wangari Maathai is an excellent example of a disruptive environmental leader:

1. **Challenging the Status Quo:** Wangari Maathai challenged the status quo by advocating for the intersectionality of environmental issues with social justice. She recognized that environmental degradation disproportionately affects marginalized communities and advocated for their inclusion in decision-making processes. She empowered women to take action and make a difference by planting trees and restoring degraded land, challenging traditional gender roles.

2. **Promoting Grassroots Empowerment:** Maathai's Green Belt Movement empowered communities to take ownership of their environment and work towards its restoration. By empowering women to plant trees, she created a movement that engaged communities in environmental stewardship and redefined traditional conservation practices.

3. **Advocating for Environmental Justice:** Wangari Maathai was a fierce advocate for environmental justice. She recognized the disproportionate impact of environmental degradation on marginalized communities, particularly women and children, and called for equal access to natural resources. Her activism inspired an environmental justice movement that continues to fight for equity and sustainability around the world.

4. **Developing Innovative Solutions:** Maathai developed innovative solutions to environmental problems. Her Green Belt Movement planted over 50 million trees across Kenya and

provided women with a source of income through tree nurseries. Her approach to conservation integrated environmental, social and economic factors to develop sustainable solutions.

5. **Inspiring Global Action:** Wangari Maathai's leadership inspired a global movement for environmental justice and sustainability. Her work has influenced environmental policies and practices across Africa and beyond. Her legacy lives on in the Green Belt Movement, which continues to plant trees and empower communities to take action towards sustainable development.

In conclusion, Wangari Maathai was an exceptional environmental leader who challenged the status quo and advocated for environmental justice and grassroots empowerment. She developed innovative solutions to environmental problems and inspired a global movement for sustainability. Her leadership serves as an inspiration to all who strive to make a positive impact on the environment and promote social justice.

3.8 Environmental Leaders Break the Mold

Environmental leaders come in all shapes and sizes, and they often break the mold of traditional leadership roles. The SPEND framework - which categorizes environmental leaders into superheroes, politicians, earth stewards, nerds, and disruptors - provides a good starting point for understanding the diverse range of skills and qualities that environmental leadership requires. However, many environmental leaders have overlapping qualities, and it's important to decide which path you want to take as an environmental leader.

Each category in the SPEND framework represents a different approach to environmental leadership. Superheroes, for example, are driven by a relentless belief in righting environmental injustices, while politicians use their power and influence to drive policy change. Earth stewards see environmental stewardship as a personal and spiritual responsibility, while nerds focus on the details and use their expertise to drive action. Disruptors challenge the status quo and use innovative approaches to drive change.

It's important to understand the strengths and limitations of each approach and to decide which path aligns most closely with your interests and skills. For example, if you're passionate about working with communities and empowering them to take action towards environmental justice, the earth steward path might be the best fit for you. If you're interested in using data and analysis to drive policy change, the nerd path might be a better fit.

However, it's also important to recognize that many environmental leaders have overlapping qualities. A politician can also be a disruptor, using their power and influence to challenge the status quo. A nerd can also be a superhero, using their expertise to fight for environmental justice. By recognizing and embracing these overlapping qualities, environmental leaders can develop a broader skill set and become more effective agents of change.

Regardless of which path you choose, there are certain characteristics of the SPEND framework that can support your development as an environmental leader. Superheroes can benefit from developing their courage and determination, while politicians can benefit from developing their communication and negotiation skills. Earth stewards can benefit from developing their spiritual and moral grounding, while nerds can benefit from developing their ability to communicate complex information in a compelling way. Disruptors can benefit from developing their innovation and creativity.

Environmental leaders break the mold of traditional leadership roles and come in a wide range of shapes and sizes. The SPEND framework provides a useful starting point for understanding the diverse range of skills and qualities that environmental leadership requires. By deciding which path aligns most closely with your interests and skills and embracing overlapping qualities, you can develop a broader skill set and become a more effective agent of change.

3.8.1   Reflection Questions

1. Which category in the SPEND framework resonates with me the most? Why?

2. Can I identify any overlapping qualities between the different categories in the SPEND framework? How can I leverage these qualities to become a more effective environmental leader?

3. What are the key skills and qualities required for success in my chosen path of environmental leadership (e.g. earth steward, disruptor, politician)? How can I develop these skills?

4. How can I use the SPEND framework to better understand the strengths and limitations of different approaches to environmental leadership?

5. In what ways can I collaborate with individuals who have a different approach to environmental leadership than me (e.g. a superhero collaborating with an earth steward)? How can we leverage our unique skills and qualities to drive positive change?

6. How can I continue to learn from and be inspired by environmental leaders in all categories of the SPEND framework?

7. What can I learn from unique approaches and perspectives from other environmental advocates?

8. Is there anyone I look up to that fits one of the SPEND categories?

9. What scares me about the SPEND framework? How can I face those fears?

10. What's the most exciting thing about choosing an environmental leadership path?

---

4 CORE COMPETENCIES OF EFFECTIVE ENVIRONMENTAL LEADERS

Effective environmental leadership requires a range of competencies and qualities that enable leaders to inspire and mobilize action, build coalitions, and achieve sustainable outcomes. Here are some of the core competencies and qualities of effective environmental leaders:

4.1 VISION AND STRATEGIC THINKING

One of the most important competencies for effective environmental leaders is the ability to articulate a clear and compelling vision for a sustainable future. This requires the ability to think creatively and long-term, anticipate future trends and challenges, and identify opportunities for positive change.

4.1.1 Having a clear vision

A clear and compelling vision helps to inspire action and galvanize support from stakeholders. It provides a roadmap for achieving sustainability and helps to guide decision-making at all levels. Effective environmental leaders are able to communicate this vision in a way that resonates with people and motivates them to take action.

4.1.2 Strategic thinking

In addition to a clear vision, effective environmental leaders must also be skilled in strategic thinking. This means being able to develop a comprehensive and actionable plan for achieving their vision. They must be able to assess the current state of affairs, identify potential obstacles and opportunities, and develop a plan that maximizes the chances of success.

4.1.3 Using your crystal ball

Strategic thinking also requires the ability to anticipate future trends and challenges. Effective environmental leaders must be able to identify emerging issues and develop strategies to address them proactively. This requires a deep understanding of the complex systems that underlie environmental problems, as well as the political, economic, and social factors that influence them.

4.1.4 Work together

To be successful in developing a clear vision and strategic plan, environmental leaders must be able to collaborate effectively with others. This requires strong communication and interpersonal skills, as well as the ability to build trust and engage stakeholders in a meaningful way.

The ability to articulate a clear and compelling vision for a sustainable future and develop a strategic plan to achieve that vision is a core competency of effective environmental leaders. This requires the ability to think creatively and long-term, anticipate future trends and challenges, and identify opportunities for positive change. Successful environmental leaders are able to communicate their vision effectively, collaborate with others, and develop actionable plans that guide decision-making at all levels.

4.2   COURAGE AND RISK-TAKING

Effective environmental leaders must be willing to take risks and make bold decisions in the face of adversity. They should be willing to challenge the status quo, advocate for unpopular causes, and speak truth to power.

4.2.1   Developing courage

Courage is essential for environmental leadership because it often requires standing up against powerful interests and entrenched systems. It takes courage to challenge the status quo and advocate for change, even when it is unpopular or goes against conventional wisdom.

4.2.2   Taking risks

Risk-taking is also an important part of environmental leadership. Successful environmental leaders are willing to take calculated risks in pursuit of their goals. This means being willing to try new approaches, take on ambitious projects, and explore uncharted territories.

However, risk-taking requires careful consideration of potential outcomes and consequences. Effective environmental leaders are able to weigh the risks and benefits of different courses of action and make informed decisions based on their analysis.

4.2.3   Being adaptable

In addition to courage and risk-taking, effective environmental leaders must also be able to persevere in the face of challenges and setbacks. Environmental issues can be complex and multifaceted, and progress can be slow and difficult to achieve. Leaders must be able to stay focused on their goals and maintain a positive outlook, even when facing significant obstacles.

To develop courage and risk-taking skills, environmental leaders must be willing to step out of their comfort zones and take on new challenges. This means being open to feedback and constructive criticism, as well as seeking out opportunities for growth and learning.

Courage and risk-taking are essential competencies for effective environmental leaders. Leaders must be willing to challenge the status quo, advocate for unpopular causes, and take calculated risks in pursuit of their goals. By developing these skills and persevering in the face of challenges, environmental leaders can drive positive change and create a more sustainable future.

4.3   COLLABORATION AND PARTNERSHIP BUILDING

Effective environmental leaders must be able to work with diverse stakeholders, build inclusive coalitions, and foster partnerships across sectors and domains. This requires strong collaboration and partnership-building skills, including conflict resolution, negotiation, and consensus-building.

4.3.1   Listening to everyone

Collaboration and partnership building are essential for environmental leadership because many environmental issues are complex and multifaceted, requiring input and expertise from a range of stakeholders. Leaders must be able to work effectively with individuals and groups from different backgrounds, cultures, and perspectives to develop solutions that are equitable and sustainable.

4.3.2   Building trust

Effective collaboration also requires the ability to build trust among stakeholders and create a shared sense of purpose and vision. Leaders must be skilled at active listening, communicating clearly and transparently, and finding common ground to bridge differences and build consensus.

4.3.3   Leveraging resources

Partnership building is also important for environmental leaders because it enables them to leverage resources and expertise from a wide range of sources. Leaders must be able to identify potential partners and allies, build relationships with them, and foster a culture of cooperation and collaboration.

To develop collaboration and partnership-building skills, environmental leaders can seek out opportunities for experiential learning, such as participating in cross-cultural exchanges or engaging in community-based projects. They can also seek out mentors or role models who exemplify strong collaboration and partnership-building skills and learn from their experiences.

Collaboration and partnership building are essential competencies for effective environmental leaders. Leaders must be able to work effectively with diverse stakeholders, build inclusive coalitions, and foster partnerships across sectors and domains.

4.4   EMPATHY AND COMMUNICATION SKILLS

Effective environmental leaders should have strong communication skills and be able to empathize with perspectives and views. This requires the ability to listen actively, build trust, and communicate ideas and goals clearly and persuasively to diverse audiences.

4.4.1   Empathy

Empathy is essential for environmental leadership because it enables leaders to understand and connect with people from different backgrounds and cultures. Leaders must be able to put themselves in other people's shoes and see issues from multiple perspectives to develop solutions that are equitable and sustainable.

4.4.2   Communication skills

Strong communication skills are also critical for environmental leaders. Leaders must be able to articulate their ideas and goals clearly and persuasively to different audiences, including policymakers, stakeholders, and the general public. They must be able to communicate complex information in a way that is easy to understand and compelling.

4.4.3   Listening for real

Effective communication also requires the ability to build trust and establish rapport with stakeholders. This means being able to listen actively, seek out feedback, and respond to concerns in a respectful and constructive way. It also means being transparent and honest in communications, even when the message may be difficult or unpopular.

To develop empathy and communication skills, environmental leaders can seek out opportunities for cultural exchange and immersion, engage in active listening and mindfulness practices, and practice effective communication techniques such as effective writing and public speaking.

Empathy and communication skills are essential competencies for effective environmental leaders. Leaders must be able to empathize with different perspectives and connect with people from diverse backgrounds, as well as communicate their ideas and goals clearly and persuasively to a range of stakeholders.

4.5 ADAPTABILITY AND RESILIENCE

Effective environmental leaders must be able to adapt to changing circumstances and respond to new challenges and opportunities. They should be resilient in the face of setbacks and failures, learn from experience, and continue to innovate and improve.

4.5.1 Adaptability

Adaptability is essential for environmental leadership because environmental issues are constantly evolving, and leaders must be able to respond quickly and effectively to new challenges and opportunities. Leaders must be able to think creatively and explore new solutions as circumstances change, even if this means departing from traditional practices or approaches.

4.5.2 Resilience

Resilience is also important for environmental leaders because progress towards sustainability can be slow and challenging. Setbacks and failures are common, and leaders must be able to bounce back quickly, learn from experience, and stay motivated despite setbacks.

Effective environmental leaders are able to cultivate resilience by taking a growth mindset approach to challenges and failures. They view setbacks as opportunities to learn and grow, and use feedback and constructive criticism to improve their skills and approaches.

4.5.3 Inspiration

In addition to adaptability and resilience, effective environmental leaders must also be able to inspire and motivate others to adapt and innovate. This requires strong leadership skills, including the ability to create a shared sense of purpose and vision, build trust, and empower others to take ownership of their work and contribute to collective goals.

To develop adaptability and resilience skills, environmental leaders can seek out opportunities for experiential learning, such as participating in innovation labs or engaging in trial-and-error approaches to problem-solving. They can also practice mindfulness and self-care techniques to build resilience and maintain a positive outlook in the face of adversity.

Adaptability and resilience are essential competencies for effective environmental leaders. Leaders must be able to adapt to changing circumstances, respond to new challenges and opportunities, and cultivate resilience in the face of setbacks and failures.

4.6 ETHICS AND ACCOUNTABILITY

Effective environmental leaders should be guided by ethical principles and values such as honesty, integrity, and transparency. They should be accountable to their stakeholders and the public and work to ensure that environmental decisions are made in a fair, equitable, and just manner.

4.6.1 Ethics

Ethics is essential for environmental leadership because environmental issues often involve complex trade-offs and competing interests. Leaders must be able to make decisions that are grounded in sound ethical principles and values, such as the intrinsic value of nature, environmental justice, and intergenerational equity.

4.6.2 Transparency

Transparency is also important for environmental leaders because it helps to build trust and establish credibility with stakeholders. Leaders must be willing to disclose information and engage in open and honest dialogue with stakeholders and the public.

4.6.3 Taking responsibility

Effective environmental leaders are accountable to their stakeholders and the public, including future generations. They must be willing to take responsibility for their actions and decisions, and work to ensure that environmental decisions are made in a fair, equitable, and just manner.

To develop ethics and accountability skills, environmental leaders can seek out opportunities for training and education in ethics, participate in ethical decision-making processes, and practice transparency and accountability in all aspects of their work.

Ethics and accountability are essential competencies for effective environmental leaders. Leaders must be guided by ethical principles and values, be accountable to their stakeholders and the public, and work to ensure that environmental decisions are made in a fair, equitable, and just manner.

4.7 EQUITY AND ACCESSIBILITY

Effective environmental leaders should strive to be equitable and accessible. This means they need to include diverse voices and perspectives in decision-making and create opportunities for marginalized communities to participate in environmental policy and planning.

4.7.1 Social justice

Equity and social justice are essential for environmental leadership because environmental issues often have disproportionate impacts on marginalized communities. Leaders must be able to recognize and address these inequities by actively engaging with affected communities, listening to their concerns and needs, and working to ensure that they have an equal voice in decision-making processes.

4.7.2   Accessibility

Accessibility is also important for environmental leaders because it helps to ensure that all stakeholders can participate in environmental policy and planning. Leaders must be able to create inclusive processes that allow for participation from individuals with diverse backgrounds and abilities.

4.7.3   Prioritizing needs

Effective environmental leaders work to achieve equity and accessibility by prioritizing the needs of marginalized communities and incorporating their perspectives into decision-making processes. They must be willing to challenge existing power structures and advocate for change that benefits disadvantaged groups.

To develop equity and accessibility skills, environmental leaders can seek out opportunities to engage with diverse communities and learn about their unique environmental challenges and concerns. Leaders can also educate themselves on issues related to environmental justice and incorporate equity considerations into their decision-making processes.

Equity and accessibility are essential competencies for effective environmental leaders. Leaders must prioritize the needs of marginalized communities, create inclusive decision-making processes, and work towards creating a more just and inclusive society.

Effective environmental leadership requires a range of competencies and qualities that enable leaders to inspire and mobilize action, build coalitions, and achieve sustainable outcomes. The core competencies we have explored include courage and risk-taking, collaboration and partnership-building, empathy and communication skills, adaptability and resilience, ethics and accountability, and equity and accessibility.

By cultivating these competencies and qualities, environmental leaders can drive positive change and make a lasting impact on the world. They can inspire and mobilize others to take action towards a more sustainable future, build coalitions that cross boundaries and sectors, and achieve sustainable outcomes that benefit all members of society.

Effective environmental leaders are not only passionate and committed to their work, they are also adaptable, strategic, and collaborative in their approach. They recognize the complexity and interdependence of environmental issues, and they work to address these challenges in a way that is equitable, transparent, and just.

To develop these competencies and qualities, environmental leaders must be willing to step out of their comfort zones, seek out opportunities for growth and learning, and engage with diverse communities and perspectives. They must be committed to ongoing self-reflection and improvement, and be willing to challenge their own assumptions and biases.

4.8 CHALLENGES AND OPPORTUNITIES OF ENVIRONMENTAL LEADERSHIP

Effective environmental leadership is not without its challenges. Leaders must navigate complex systems and stakeholders, address competing interests, and work to overcome systemic barriers that impede progress towards sustainability. However, there are also opportunities for leaders to innovate, collaborate, and drive positive change.

Environmental leaders face a variety of challenges as they work to promote sustainable practices and protect the environment. These challenges can include resistance from vested interests, lack of resources including funding and time, inadequate infrastructure, and limited expertise in navigating complex environmental issues. Furthermore, the scale and complexity of environmental problems can be overwhelming, making it difficult for leaders to know where to start or focus their efforts.

Despite these challenges, there are also opportunities for environmental leaders to drive positive change and create a more sustainable future. Technological innovation, community engagement, and collaboration with other stakeholders can provide opportunities for leaders to inspire and mobilize action.

To be effective environmental leaders, it is crucial to understand both the challenges and opportunities of this work. By developing strategies to overcome barriers and leverage opportunities, environmental leaders can build momentum towards a more sustainable future. With determination, creativity, and persistence, environmental leaders can drive positive change and make a lasting impact on the world.

4.8.1   Barriers to Environmental Leadership

Environmental leaders face a range of challenges that can impede progress towards sustainability. These barriers can include resistance from vested interests, lack of resources, inadequate infrastructure, and limited expertise.

4.8.1.1   *Resistance from Vested Interests*

One of the major barriers to environmental leadership is resistance from powerful stakeholders who may feel threatened by changes that could impact their profits or power. This can include corporations or governments who prioritize economic growth over environmental protection, or individuals who resist changes that challenge their beliefs or values.

Leaders who face this barrier must be prepared to push back against resistance, often through advocacy and lobbying efforts. They may need to form coalitions and collaborate with other stakeholders who share their goals and values. Building strong partnerships means using influence to advocate for policies that prioritize sustainability. Environmental leaders can overcome these barriers and drive positive change.

4.8.1.2   *Lack of Resources*

Environmental leaders often face inadequacies in terms of funding, time, and emotional support. This can limit their effectiveness in driving meaningful change, as they may not have the necessary resources to address complex environmental issues.

To overcome this barrier, leaders may need to seek out alternative sources of funding, such as grants or private sector partnerships. They may also need to prioritize their work and focus on areas where they can make the most impact, given their available resources. Emotional support can be found by engaging with like-minded environmentalists and communities to help refresh and recharge your passion and drive.

4.8.1.3 Inadequate Infrastructure

In some cases, environmental leaders may face barriers related to inadequate infrastructure. For example, waste management facilities or public transportation systems may not be adequate to address environmental challenges in a given community. This can create further obstacles for leaders who are trying to promote sustainable practices.

To overcome this barrier, leaders may need to work with other stakeholders to advocate for improved infrastructure, such as renewable energy facilities, recycling plants, and public transit options. This may require collaboration with local governments or private companies to secure the necessary funding and resources.

4.8.1.4 Limited Expertise

Finally, leaders may face a barrier related to limited expertise in navigating complex environmental issues. Environmental sustainability requires a deep understanding of scientific data, legal frameworks, and policy initiatives. Leaders who lack this expertise may find it difficult to make informed decisions about how to address environmental challenges.

To overcome this barrier, leaders can seek out training and education opportunities that will help them develop the necessary expertise. This may include attending conferences, workshops, or seminars, or pursuing advanced degrees in relevant fields. They can also collaborate with or hire experts in areas where they need more information to make informed decisions.

Environmental leadership faces several barriers that can impede progress towards sustainability. The first step to address them is to recognize these barriers and develop strategies to overcome them. Leaders can drive positive change and create a more sustainable future with patience and wisdom. Through advocacy, collaboration, and a commitment to ongoing learning, environmental leaders can overcome these barriers and drive positive change.

4.8.2   Opportunities for Environmental Leadership

Environmental leaders have a unique opportunity to drive positive change and create a more sustainable future. By leveraging technological innovation, community engagement, and collaboration with other stakeholders, they can inspire and mobilize action towards more sustainable practices.

4.8.2.1 *Technological Innovation*

New technologies, such as renewable energy sources, smart grids, and green infrastructure, are rapidly transforming the environmental landscape. These innovations provide opportunities for environmental leaders to inspire and mobilize action towards more sustainable practices. Leaders can also leverage these technologies to showcase the benefits of environmentally-friendly practices and encourage individuals and organizations to adopt sustainable practices.

By staying up-to-date with advances in technology and engaging with innovators in this space, environmental leaders can stay ahead of the curve and be well-positioned to drive positive change.

4.8.2.2 *Community Engagement*

Environmental leaders can leverage community participation and support to build stronger coalitions and drive change at the grassroots level. By engaging with local communities, leaders can gain a deeper understanding of their needs and concerns, and work to address environmental issues in a way that is culturally-sensitive and inclusive. This allows leaders to build trust and establish credibility with stakeholders, which can be key to driving long-term change.

Leaders can engage with communities in a variety of ways, including through outreach campaigns, community events, and participatory decision-making processes. By empowering individuals and organizations to take an active role in environmental sustainability, leaders can drive meaningful progress and create a more sustainable future.

4.8.2.3   Collaboration

Environmental leaders can work with other stakeholders, including businesses and governments, to create partnerships and drive collective action. By collaborating with other organizations, leaders can pool resources, share expertise, and drive change at a larger scale. Collaborations can take many forms, including public-private partnerships, multi-stakeholder initiatives, and cross-sectoral projects.

Effective collaborations require leaders to be skilled in communication, negotiation, and conflict resolution. By building strong relationships with other stakeholders and fostering a culture of trust and mutual respect, leaders can create partnerships that drive positive change and promote sustainable practices.

Environmental leadership provides numerous opportunities for leaders to drive positive change and create a more sustainable future. By leveraging technological innovation, engaging with local communities, and collaborating with other stakeholders, leaders can inspire and mobilize action towards more sustainable practices. Embrace these, and environmental leaders will make a lasting impact towards a more sustainable future.

4.8.3   Strategies for Overcoming Challenges and Leveraging Opportunities

Environmental leaders face numerous challenges as they work to promote sustainable practices and protect the environment. At the same time, there are also many opportunities for leaders to innovate, collaborate, and drive positive change. Leaders must develop effective strategies for overcoming barriers and leveraging opportunities.

4.8.3.1   *Building Coalitions*

One of the most effective strategies for environmental leadership is building coalitions. By working with diverse stakeholders and building inclusive coalitions, environmental leaders can amplify their impact and overcome systemic barriers to progress. Leaders can bring together individuals and organizations with shared values and goals, creating a sense of collective purpose that drives meaningful change. This approach allows leaders to tap into the strengths and resources of different groups, building momentum towards larger goals.

4.8.3.2   *Advocacy and Lobbying*

Another key strategy for environmental leadership is advocacy and lobbying. Leaders can use their influence and platforms to advocate for policies and laws that promote sustainable practices and protect the environment. By engaging with policymakers and other decision-makers, leaders can shape public opinion and drive policy change at local, national, and international levels. Effective advocacy requires leaders to be skilled in communication, negotiation, and persuasion, and to be well-informed about current issues and trends.

4.8.3.3   *Innovation and Experimentation*

Finally, leaders can experiment with new approaches to environmental sustainability, embracing trial-and-error methodologies to find what works best in their context. By taking risks and trying out new ideas, leaders can learn from their successes and failures and create more effective strategies over time. Innovation can come in many forms, such as developing new technologies or business models, exploring alternative funding sources, or creating new partnerships and collaborations.

Effective environmental leadership requires careful strategy development, including building coalitions, advocacy and lobbying, and innovation and experimentation. By adopting these strategies, leaders can overcome barriers and leverage opportunities to promote sustainable practices, protect the environment, and advance social justice. Environmental leadership is a crucial tool in creating a more sustainable and just world, today.

4.9 CONCLUSION

This chapter has explored the challenges and opportunities of environmental leadership, highlighting the importance of this work in addressing environmental challenges and creating a more sustainable future. First, we looked at the core competencies of environmental leadership: vision, courage, collaboration, empathy, adaptability, ethics, and equity. Then, we examined the barriers that environmental leaders face, including resistance from vested interests, lack of resources, inadequate infrastructure, and limited expertise. Finally, we have explored the opportunities for environmental leadership, including technological innovation, community engagement, and collaboration with other stakeholders.

To overcome these barriers and leverage these opportunities, effective environmental leaders must develop a range of competencies and qualities. These include courage and risk-taking, collaboration and partnership-building, empathy and communication skills, adaptability and resilience, ethics and accountability, and equity and accessibility. By cultivating these core competencies, environmental leaders can inspire and mobilize action, build coalitions, and achieve sustainable outcomes.

Effective environmental leadership is crucial to achieving a more sustainable and just world. Environmental leaders play a vital role in protecting the natural environment, promoting sustainable practices, and advancing social justice.

You must embrace environmental leadership in your own communities, whether through advocacy, collaboration, or innovation. Let's work together to address environmental challenges, and create a more sustainable and just world for ourselves and future generations.

4.10 REFLECTION QUESTIONS

1. What are some of the core competencies of effective environmental leadership, and how can they be developed?

2. What are some of the barriers that environmental leaders face, and what strategies can be used to overcome them?

3. Why is it important for environmental leaders to embrace vision, courage, collaboration, empathy, adaptability, ethics, and equity?

4. How can environmental leaders effectively communicate with stakeholders who may resist change or have conflicting interests?

5. What role does community engagement play in environmental leadership, and how can leaders effectively engage with local communities?

6. How can environmental leaders leverage technological innovation to drive positive change and promote sustainable practices?

7. How can leaders effectively collaborate with other stakeholders, including businesses and governments, to create partnerships that drive collective action?

8. Why is experimentation and innovation important in environmental leadership, and how can leaders effectively experiment with new approaches to sustainability?

9. How can individuals who are not currently in leadership roles develop and cultivate skills that are necessary for environmental leadership?

10. Why is it crucial for environmental leaders to prioritize social justice and equity in their work, and how can they ensure that their efforts are inclusive and accessible to all members of society?

11. SUPPLEMENTARY ACTIVITIES

12. **Self-Assessment Activity:** Use a self-assessment tool, such as the Environmental Leadership Capacity Inventory (ELCI), to assess your current level of environmental leadership capacity. This tool can help identify areas where you may need to improve and provide guidance on how to develop core competencies. After completing the assessment, reflect on the results and develop a plan for enhancing your skills.

13. **Mentorship Program:** Seek out a mentor who has experience in environmental leadership and community engagement. This could be a professional in your field, a community leader, or an academic advisor. Meet with your mentor regularly to discuss challenges, share ideas, and receive feedback on your progress. This activity helps to develop new skills and insights while building a supportive network.

14. **Volunteer Project:** Find a local environmental organization or community group that aligns with your values and interests. Volunteer your time and skills to support their mission, and look for opportunities to take on leadership roles within the organization. This activity provides valuable hands-on experience in environmental leadership and community engagement, while helping to create positive change in your local community.

4.10.1 The Environmental Leadership Capacity Inventory

Instructions: For each item, indicate the extent to which it describes your current behavior or skill set using the following scale:

- 0 - Not at all
- 1 - Somewhat
- 2 - Moderately
- 3 - Very much
- 4 - To a great extent

____ 1. I have a clear vision of what I want to achieve in the field of environmental leadership. ____ 2. I am willing to take risks and make difficult decisions to achieve my goals. ____ 3. I am able to build and maintain positive relationships with stakeholders from diverse backgrounds. ____ 4. I am able to communicate effectively with individuals and groups, both verbally and in writing. ____ 5. I am able to adapt to changing circumstances and respond to new challenges. ____ 6. I am committed to ethical values and practices, and hold myself accountable for my actions. ____ 7. I consistently work to promote social justice and equity in my environmental leadership efforts. ____ 8. I am able to collaborate effectively with other stakeholders, including businesses, government agencies, and community organizations. ____ 9. I am able to engage and inspire others to take action on environmental issues. ____ 10. I am able to identify and leverage opportunities for positive change in the environmental field.

Scoring: Add up your total score out of a possible 40 points. Higher scores indicate greater capacity for environmental leadership.

Interpretation:

- **0-10:** Low capacity for environmental leadership. Consider focusing on developing core competencies through training, mentorship, and networking opportunities.

- **11-20:** Some capacity for environmental leadership. Focus on developing specific competencies where improvement is needed.

- **21-30:** Moderate capacity for environmental leadership. Continue to develop key competencies and seek out leadership opportunities to enhance skills.

- **31-40:** High capacity for environmental leadership. Utilize your skills and experiences to drive positive change and mentor others in developing environmental leadership capacity.

  After completing the assessment, reflect on your results. Identify areas where you scored lower and develop a plan for enhancing those competencies. Seek out training, mentorship opportunities, and networking events to continue building your environmental leadership capacity. Consider setting specific goals and timelines for improvement, and track your progress over time. Remember that environmental leadership is a continuous journey of self-improvement and growth.

5 BASIC ENVIRONMENTAL KNOWLEDGE

Environmental knowledge is the understanding of the natural world, its resources, and the impact that humans have on it. It encompasses scientific principles, policy frameworks, cultural values, and community perspectives. These shape our relationship with the environment. Developing environmental knowledge means gaining a deeper understanding of these complex issues and their interconnections.

In today's world, environmental challenges are becoming increasingly urgent and complex. Climate change, biodiversity loss, pollution, and resource depletion are just a few of the pressing problems. These require effective environmental leadership and action. Developing environmental knowledge is crucial for individuals who want to make a positive impact on these issues, whether through community engagement, policy advocacy, or professional work. By building a strong foundation of environmental knowledge, individuals can better understand the challenges at hand, identify opportunities for positive change, and communicate effectively with diverse stakeholders.

I've had a few colleagues who have acquired their environmental knowledge by lived experience, and not by book learning. They often feel "less-than" people like me, who have had access to formal education. This is a cultural myth. Your knowledge of the environment is valuable regardless of how you acquire it.

If you are younger or have recently joined an environmental group, you may be more subject to this bias. Luckily, there are plenty of opportunities for you to both gain new knowledge, and make sure that your partners and coworkers respect the knowledge that you've arrived with.

In this section, we will explore strategies for developing environmental knowledge and staying informed about the latest research and best practices. We will examine the key concepts and issues in environmental science and in local communities, as well as various resources and tools for staying informed and communicating effectively.

We will also discuss the importance of networking and collaboration in developing environmental knowledge. By the end of this section, you will have gained practical insights into how to build your own environmental knowledge and become a more effective environmental leader.

5.1 KEY CONCEPTS AND ISSUES IN ENVIRONMENTAL SCIENCE AND IN YOUR LOCAL COMMUNITY

The world we live in is complex and interconnected. There are many different systems and processes at work. Environmental science is the study of these systems and processes, and how they are impacted by human activities. Understanding the key concepts and issues in environmental science is crucial for individuals who want to make a positive impact on the world around them.

Environmental science is a combination field. What I mean is that it's made up of little bits and pieces of other formal studies. You might use a concept from biology, chemistry, or physics to shine light on an issue. Psychology and sociology also come into play. It's messy - and that's ok.

One reason why it's important to understand environmental science is to gain a deeper understanding of the major environmental issues facing the world today. Climate change, biodiversity loss, pollution, and resource depletion are just a few of the pressing problems that require effective environmental leadership and action. By understanding the underlying causes and impacts of these issues, we can better identify opportunities for positive change.

Another important reason to understand environmental science is to better appreciate the natural world and our place in it. Environmental science teaches us about the intricate relationships between different species, the fundamental principles of energy and matter cycling, and the role of ecosystems in sustaining life on Earth. But we must internalize and apply this knowledge. Gaining a deeper appreciation for the natural world helps your sense of connection and responsibility toward the planet and its inhabitants.

Understanding environmental science is also important at the local level. Local communities face a range of environmental challenges, from air and water pollution to land use change and ecosystem degradation. Your local community is facing unique environmental challenges. When you understand the science, you can better identify and address these problems within your own communities. This can involve conducting local environmental assessments, collecting data and analyzing trends, engaging with stakeholders, and developing prioritization plans.

Understanding the key concepts and issues in environmental science is crucial for anyone who wants to make a positive impact on the world around them. It helps us to better understand the major environmental challenges facing our planet, appreciate the natural world, and take action at the local level to address environmental issues. Your environmental leadership journey begins with acquiring basic environmental knowledge.

5.1.1 Overview of Major Environmental Issues

The world we live in is facing a number of environmental challenges. These have the potential to significantly impact the health and well-being of current and future generations. All of these challenges are complex and interrelated, but they can be broadly categorized into seven major environmental issues: climate change, biodiversity loss, pollution, resource depletion, land use change, water scarcity, and food security.

5.1.1.1 *Climate Change*

Climate change is caused by the buildup of greenhouse gases in the atmosphere, primarily from the burning of fossil fuels such as coal, oil, and gas. This can lead to rising temperatures, changing weather patterns, and sea level rise, with potentially catastrophic impacts on ecosystems, food systems, and human health and well-being.

5.1.1.1.1 Suggested Reading

1. "This Changes Everything: Capitalism vs. The Climate" by Naomi Klein - This book examines how the climate crisis is linked to capitalism and explores ways to create a more equitable and sustainable future.

2. "The Sixth Extinction" by Elizabeth Kolbert - This book looks at how human activity has caused mass extinctions in the past and how it is currently causing the sixth mass extinction of species on Earth.

3. "Climate Change: What Everyone Needs to Know" by Joseph Romm - This book provides an overview of climate change, from its causes and effects to potential solutions for mitigating its impacts.

4. "Don't Even Think About It: Why Our Brains Are Wired To Ignore Climate Change" by George Marshall - This book examines why people often ignore or deny climate change despite overwhelming evidence of its existence and impact on our planet.

5. "The Ministry for the Future" by Kim Stanley Robinson - This novel follows a fictional United Nations agency created to address climate change and other global challenges facing humanity in the near future.

5.1.1.2   *Biodiversity Loss*

Biodiversity is the variety of life on Earth, including all species of plants, animals, and microorganisms, as well as the genetic diversity within each species. Biodiversity loss is caused by habitat destruction, overexploitation of resources, pollution, and climate change. This loss of biodiversity can lead to disruption of ecosystems, reduced resilience to environmental stresses, and potential loss of important medicines and other natural products.

5.1.1.2.1   Suggested Reading

1. "The Diversity of Life" by Edward O. Wilson - A comprehensive look at the variety of life on Earth and how it is being threatened by human activities.

2. "The Song of the Dodo" by David Quammen - An exploration into the causes and consequences of species extinction, with a focus on island biogeography and ecology.

3. "Nature's Best Hope" by Doug Tallamy - A call to action for individuals to make a difference in conserving biodiversity through their own backyards and gardens, using native plants as part of the solution to saving species from extinction.

4. "Wild Hope: On the Front Lines of Conservation Success" by Andrew Balmford - This book offers a more hopeful perspective on conservation efforts, highlighting examples of successful projects that have helped to protect and restore biodiversity in various parts of the world.

5.1.1.3   *Pollution*

Pollution refers to the presence or introduction of harmful substances into the environment that can cause harm to humans, animals, and ecosystems. This can include air pollution from transportation and industry, water pollution from agricultural and industrial runoff, and soil pollution from chemical contaminants.

1.   "Breath Taking: The Power, Fragility, and Future of Our Extraordinary Lungs" by Michael J. Stephen - This book focuses on air pollution and its impacts on human respiratory health, as well as potential solutions for reducing pollution and protecting lung health.

2.   "Plastic: A Toxic Love Story" by Susan Freinkel - This book explores the ubiquitous presence of plastic in our lives and its impacts on human health and the environment.

3.   "Garbage Land: On the Secret Trail of Trash" by Elizabeth Royte - This book investigates the complex world of waste management and the environmental impacts of trash disposal.

4.   "Guns, Germs, and Steel: The Fates of Human Societies" by Jared Diamond - An exploration into how geography, technology, and biology have shaped human societies throughout history and their effects on pollution.

5.   "Silent Spring" by Rachel Carson - An eye-opening look at the effects of chemical pesticides on nature and humanity, inspiring an environmental movement that changed our relationship with pollution.

5.1.1.4   Resource Depletion

Resource depletion refers to the exhaustion of natural resources, such as fossil fuels, minerals, and timber. This can lead to economic instability, social conflict, and environmental degradation, as well as potential impacts on human health and well-being.

1.   "The End of Nature" by Bill McKibben - This book explores the impact of human activities, including the depletion of natural resources, on the Earth's ecosystems.

2. "The Limits to Growth: A Report for the Club of Rome's Project on the Predicament of Mankind" by Donella H. Meadows, Jorgen Randers, and Dennis L. Meadows - This influential book examines the potential consequences of unchecked resource depletion and population growth.

3. "Collapse: How Societies Choose to Fail or Succeed" by Jared Diamond - This book looks at how environmental factors, including resource depletion, have contributed to the collapse of societies throughout history.

4. "The Conundrum: How Scientific Innovation, Increased Efficiency, and Good Intentions Can Make Our Energy and Climate Problems Worse" by David Owen - This book explores the paradox of increased efficiency leading to greater resource consumption, particularly in relation to energy and climate issues.

5. "Energy and Civilization: A History" by Vaclav Smil - This comprehensive book traces the history of energy production and consumption from pre-industrial times to the present day, with a focus on the challenges of resource depletion and sustainability.

5.1.1.5 Land Use Change

Land use change refers to the conversion of natural habitats, such as forests and wetlands, into urban or agricultural areas. This can result in loss of biodiversity, soil degradation, and increased greenhouse gas emissions.

5.1.1.5.1 Suggested Reading

1. "Changes in the Land: Indians, Colonists, and the Ecology of New England" by William Cronon - This book explores how the arrival of European settlers in North America led to significant changes in land use and ecology.

2. "The Big Ratchet: How Humanity Thrives in the Face of Natural Crisis" by Ruth DeFries - This book examines how human

societies have adapted to changing environmental conditions, including changes in land use.

3. "1491: New Revelations of the Americas Before Columbus" by Charles C. Mann - This book challenges traditional views of pre-Columbian America and explores how indigenous cultures managed and shaped the land.

4. "Dirt: The Erosion of Civilizations" by David R. Montgomery - This book examines the long history of soil erosion and its impacts on human societies and ecosystems.

5. "The Global Forest: Forty Ways Trees Can Save Us" by Diana Beresford-Kroeger - While not solely focused on land use change, this book highlights the importance of forests in maintaining healthy ecosystems and mitigating the impacts of climate change.

5.1.1.6 *Water Scarcity*

Water scarcity refers to a lack of access to clean and safe water for drinking, sanitation, and other uses. This can be caused by overuse of water resources, pollution, and climate change, and can have significant impacts on human health and well-being, as well as economic activity and social stability.

5.1.1.6.1 Suggested Reading

1. "Where The Water Goes" by David Owen - A book about the storied and complex history of water usage along the Colorado River.

2. "The Big Thirst" by Charles Fishman - A book about the history of water, as weird as that sounds.

3. "When The Rivers Run Dry" by Fred Pearce - Another look at the Colorado and other rivers as we struggle with the world's water crisis.

4. "The Poisoned City" by Anna Clark - Learn about Flint, Michigan's problems with water in this prize-winning book from a journalist.

5. "Water Wars: Privatization, Pollution, and Profit" by Vandana Shiva - An analysis of the privatization of water resources around the world, its effects on pollution levels, and how it benefits corporations over people.

5.1.1.7 *Food Security*

Food security refers to the ability of people to access sufficient, safe, and nutritious food to meet their dietary needs and preferences. This can be impacted by climate change, land use change, water scarcity, and other environmental factors, as well as social and economic factors such as poverty, inequality, and conflict.

5.1.1.7.1 Suggested Reading

1. "I Was Hungry" by Jeremy Everett - One in eight Americans struggle with food, this book offers an assessment of the current crisis and some solutions.

2. "The Town That Food Saved" by Ben Hewitt - A book about Hardwick, Vermont's relationship with food and self sustainability.

3. "The Third Plate" by Dan Barber - The author argues that the "farm to table" movement has done little to change how we eat, and provides an alternative.

4. "The Urban Food Revolution" by Peter Ladner - Reliance on industrial agriculture is causing a lot of issues. This author wants to fix it.

5. "Closing The Food Gap" by Mark Winne - How do people who can't make healthier choices deal with food and nutrition? How can we make healthy food available to everyone?

These seven major environmental issues are all interconnected and require systemic solutions in order to mitigate their impacts. By understanding these issues and their underlying causes, individuals can become more effective environmental leaders and contribute to a sustainable future for all.

5.2   UNDERSTANDING ENVIRONMENTAL SCIENCE CONCEPTS

Environmental science seeks to understand the complex interactions between humans and the natural world. It draws on a range of scientific disciplines, including biology, chemistry, geology, and physics, to explore the many ways in which human activities impact the environment.

Understanding environmental science concepts is critical for a number of reasons. First and foremost, it enables us to make informed decisions about how we interact with the natural world. From choosing energy sources to designing cities, our decisions have real-world impacts on the health of ecosystems and the well-being of all living beings.

In addition, understanding environmental science concepts helps us to appreciate the interconnectedness of all life on Earth. By recognizing the ways in which everything is connected - from the smallest microbe to the largest ecosystem - we can better appreciate the fragility and complexity of the natural world.

So what are some of the key environmental science concepts that we should strive to understand? Here's a brief overview:

- Ecosystems: Ecosystems are the foundation of life on Earth, and understanding how they work is critical for understanding ecological processes and identifying strategies for conservation and restoration.

- Energy and Matter Cycling: The flow of energy and matter through ecological systems is essential for maintaining healthy ecosystems and supporting all forms of life.

- Climate System: The climate system is complex and dynamic, and understanding its components and dynamics is essential for addressing the pressing issue of climate change.

- Biodiversity: Biodiversity refers to the variety of life on Earth, and understanding its importance and the threats to its survival is key for protecting ecosystems and promoting sustainability.

- Environmental Policy and Regulation: Policies and regulations play a critical role in shaping the choices we make as a society and in protecting the environment for future generations.

    By striving to understand these and other key environmental science concepts, we can become more effective environmental stewards and contribute to a sustainable future for all.

5.2.1 Ecosystems

Ecosystems are one of the fundamental building blocks of our natural world. Simply put, an ecosystem is a community of living organisms and the non-living components of their environment that interact with each other in a particular location. Understanding ecosystems is essential for understanding the many ways in which human activities impact the natural world and for identifying strategies for conservation and restoration.

The components of an ecosystem can be broadly divided into biotic (living) and abiotic (non-living) factors. Biotic factors include all living organisms within the ecosystem, from plants and animals to fungi and microorganisms. Abiotic factors include non-living components such as water, air, soil, rocks, and climate.

One of the key things to understand about ecosystems is the complex interactions that take place between different components. These interactions can take many different forms, from predator-prey relationships to symbiotic partnerships between different species. For example, a food web is a common way of representing the complex interactions between different organisms in an ecosystem. It shows how energy and nutrients flow through the ecosystem, from producers (such as plants) to consumers (such as herbivores and carnivores) and eventually to decomposers (such as bacteria and fungi).

Another important concept related to ecosystems is nutrient cycling. This refers to the process by which nutrients such as carbon, nitrogen, and phosphorus are cycled through the ecosystem, moving from the abiotic environment to living organisms and back again. This process is essential for maintaining the health and productivity of ecosystems.

There are many different types of ecosystems around the world, each with its own unique set of biotic and abiotic components and interactions. Some common examples include forests, oceans, grasslands, wetlands, and tundra. Each type of ecosystem has its own distinct characteristics, but all are interconnected and play an important role in the health of the planet.

Ecosystems are complex and dynamic communities of living and non-living components that interact with each other in a particular location. Understanding ecosystems is essential for understanding the many ways in which human activities impact the natural world, and for identifying strategies for conservation and restoration.

5.2.2 Energy and Matter Cycling

Energy and matter cycling are critical concepts in environmental science, as they underpin the functioning of ecosystems and the health of our planet. By understanding these concepts and their impacts on the environment, we can better appreciate the importance of sustainable resource management and conservation.

Firstly, it's important to understand the role that energy plays in ecological systems. Energy is the driving force behind all biological processes, from photosynthesis in plants to the metabolic processes of animals. Without a constant supply of energy, ecosystems would not be able to function and support life as we know it.

When it comes to energy sources, there are two main categories: renewable and non-renewable. Renewable energy sources are those that are replenished naturally over time, such as solar, wind, and hydro. Non-renewable energy sources, on the other hand, are finite and will eventually be depleted, such as fossil fuels like oil, coal, and natural gas. Understanding the difference between these two types of energy sources is crucial for developing sustainable energy systems that minimize our impact on the environment.

Another key concept related to energy and matter cycling is the carbon cycle. This refers to the movement of carbon through the Earth's atmosphere, oceans, land, and living organisms. Carbon is a key building block of life, but when too much carbon is released into the atmosphere (such as through the burning of fossil fuels), it can contribute to climate change and other environmental problems.

Similarly, the nitrogen cycle is another important process that impacts the health of ecosystems. Nitrogen is an essential nutrient for plant growth, but too much nitrogen can lead to environmental problems such as eutrophication (an excess of nutrients in water bodies) and acid rain.

Finally, the water cycle is a critical process for supporting life on Earth. Water moves through the atmosphere, oceans, and land in a continuous cycle, bringing fresh water to plants and animals and shaping the landscape over time. Understanding this process is essential for managing water resources and protecting ecosystems.

5.2.3 Climate System

The climate system is a complex and dynamic system that includes the atmosphere, hydrosphere, cryosphere, and biosphere. Understanding the components and interactions of this system is essential for addressing the pressing issue of climate change.

One of the key things to understand about the climate system is the role that human activities play in contributing to climate change. Scientists agree that the Earth's climate is changing due to human activities, such as the burning of fossil fuels and deforestation. These activities release greenhouse gases (such as carbon dioxide) into the atmosphere, which trap heat and cause the planet to warm.

The consequences of climate change are far-reaching and include rising global temperatures, melting glaciers and ice caps, sea level rise, changes in precipitation patterns, and more frequent and severe weather events. These impacts affect ecosystems, wildlife, and human societies around the world, with disproportionate impacts on vulnerable populations.

Fortunately, there are strategies for addressing climate change through both mitigation (reducing greenhouse gas emissions) and adaptation (preparing for and adapting to the impacts of climate change). Mitigation strategies include transitioning to renewable energy sources, improving energy efficiency, and promoting sustainable land use practices. Adaptation strategies include building climate-resilient infrastructure, enhancing community preparedness and response, and protecting vulnerable ecosystems.

Ultimately, addressing climate change requires a concerted global effort, with action taken at the local, national, and international levels. Governments, businesses, and individuals all have a role to play in reducing greenhouse gas emissions and preparing for the impacts of climate change.

5.2.4 Biodiversity

Biodiversity refers to the variety of life on Earth, from the smallest microbe to the largest ecosystem. It includes all living organisms and the ecosystems they inhabit, and it plays a critical role in supporting ecological processes and human well-being.

One of the key reasons that biodiversity is important is because it provides a range of ecosystem services. These include things like clean air and water, nutrient cycling, pollination, and climate regulation. Ecosystems with high levels of biodiversity are generally more resilient to environmental changes and better able to withstand disturbances such as drought, disease, and fire.

Despite its importance, biodiversity is under threat from a range of factors, including habitat loss, overexploitation, pollution, and climate change. The consequences of biodiversity loss can be severe, including impacts on ecosystem services, food security, and human health.

Fortunately, there are strategies for conserving biodiversity and promoting sustainable use of natural resources. One approach is to establish protected areas that conserve threatened ecosystems and the species that inhabit them. Habitat restoration and reforestation efforts can also help to increase biodiversity by creating new habitats and improving connectivity between existing ones.

In addition, individuals and communities can take action to support biodiversity conservation by reducing consumption, promoting sustainable agriculture practices, and supporting conservation organizations and initiatives.

5.2.5 Environmental Policy and Regulation

Environmental policy and regulation are designed to protect the natural world and promote sustainability. They serve several purposes, including setting standards for pollution control, promoting sustainable use of natural resources, and protecting public health and safety.

In the United States, environmental policy has a long history dating back to the 1960s when concerns about air and water pollution began to emerge. Since then, a range of environmental laws and regulations have been enacted at the national and state levels, including the Clean Air Act, Clean Water Act, and Endangered Species Act.

At the international level, there are also a number of agreements and treaties aimed at promoting environmental protection and sustainability, such as the Paris Agreement on climate change and the Convention on Biological Diversity.

Despite these efforts, environmental challenges continue to persist, and there is ongoing debate about the best ways to promote environmental protection and sustainability. Some argue that deregulation and market-based solutions are the most effective approach, while others advocate for stronger regulations and government intervention.

Individuals and communities also play an important role in advocating for environmental protection and policy change. This can take many forms, from participating in public comment periods and writing to elected officials to supporting environmental organizations and initiatives and making individual lifestyle changes.

5.2.6 Conclusion

Throughout this chapter, we have explored some of the key concepts and issues in environmental science. From ecosystems to energy and matter cycling, climate change to biodiversity, and environmental policy and regulation, we have seen how these concepts are interconnected and impact the health of our planet.

Understanding environmental science concepts is essential for becoming effective environmental stewards and contributing to a sustainable future for all. However, environmental challenges are complex and ongoing, and there is always more to learn and do. Continued learning and engagement with environmental issues is crucial for staying informed and taking action to protect the natural world.

Fortunately, there are many resources and opportunities available for learning and engagement, from online courses and educational materials to community organizations and advocacy groups. By staying informed and engaged, we can work together to promote sustainability and protect the health of our planet.

5.3 REFLECTION QUESTIONS

1. What were some of the key concepts and issues in environmental science that you learned about in this chapter?

2. How do these environmental science concepts impact our everyday lives, and why is it important to understand them?

3. What role do human activities play in contributing to environmental challenges such as climate change and biodiversity loss?

4. What are some of the strategies and policies that have been developed to address these challenges, and how effective have they been?

5. What are some of the challenges and obstacles to promoting sustainability and protecting the natural world, and how can we overcome them?

6. How can individuals and communities contribute to environmental protection and policy change, and what are some ways to get involved?

7. What inspires you to learn more about environmental science, and how can you continue to build your knowledge and engage with these issues?

8. What opportunities are available for learning and engagement with environmental issues in your community, and how can you take advantage of them?

9. What are some of the ethical considerations related to environmental science and sustainability, and how can we ensure that our actions align with our values?

10. How can we work together to promote sustainability and protect the health of our planet, and what role do you see yourself playing in this effort?

5.4 SUGGESTED ACTIVITIES

1. **Conduct an environmental impact assessment:** Choose a product or activity that you commonly engage in, such as driving your car or using plastic water bottles. Research the environmental impact of this activity or product, including its carbon footprint, water usage, and waste generation. Consider ways to reduce or eliminate this impact, such as using public transportation, investing in a reusable water bottle, or choosing products made from sustainable materials.

2. **Participate in a local environmental initiative or group:** Research organizations or initiatives in your community that

are working to promote sustainability and environmental protection. Attend a meeting or event, volunteer your time, or make a donation to support their work. You can also consider starting your own initiative or group focused on an environmental issue that you are passionate about.

3.   **Engage with policymakers and elected officials:** Identify local, state, or federal policymakers or elected officials who are working on environmental issues. Write a letter or email expressing your concerns and advocating for policies or regulations that promote sustainability and protect the environment. You can also participate in public comment periods or attend town hall meetings to share your views and engage in dialogue with decision-makers.

6 IDENTIFYING LOCAL ENVIRONMENTAL ISSUES

Now that we've discovered how to acquire environmental knowledge, we need to apply it. Identifying your local, homegrown environmental issues is a great place to start. This lets you work with your own community on issues that directly impact you.

Every community is different, but chances are, you already have an idea of what your community is facing. After all - you did pick up this book. Whether it's pollution or food security, you're ready to make a change.

One way you can start tackling your environmental issues is through analysis. It can be as formal or informal as you'd like. Take some time to read through this chapter, and then think about how you can apply it to your issues. Perhaps it's as simple as journaling. Perhaps it's as complex as a full scale report. No matter what you choose, getting your hands dirty will help move you from concerned citizen to environmental leader. Let's get started.

6.1 THE ENVIRONMENTAL IMPACT ASSESSMENT

Identifying local environmental issues involves conducting a local environmental assessment, which includes several steps. The first step is defining the study area and scope of the assessment, which helps to ensure that the assessment is focused and effective. For a budding environmental leader, you'll want to stick to your own neighborhood, street, or community.

The second step is identifying potential environmental issues and concerns in the local area. This can include issues such as air and water pollution, hazardous waste disposal, or soil contamination. It could be overflowing trash bins, ticks from uncut grass, eyesore houses, or the local paper plant with too much sewage run off.

The third step is collecting baseline data on environmental conditions and trends in the local area. This can involve gathering data on air and water quality, land use and zoning, demographic and socioeconomic factors, and climate and weather patterns. You may be able to use data that already exists.

The fourth step is analyzing the data to identify patterns and trends, which can help to pinpoint specific environmental issues that need to be addressed. If you don't have any statistics knowledge - that's ok. You can recruit some help, or learn online.

Stakeholder engagement is also an important part of identifying local environmental issues. This involves engaging with community members, local government officials, and environmental groups to gather input on environmental concerns and priorities.

Developing a prioritization plan is the final step in the process. This involves setting criteria for prioritization, evaluating potential solutions based on their effectiveness, feasibility, and cost, and selecting the most appropriate solutions and developing an action plan. This is your "ask" - what you want the people in power to do.

You may not complete all of these steps if you're just starting out or working solo. But engaging in the process and getting used to the lifecycle is your first big step into the shoes of an environmental leader.

Overall, identifying local environmental issues is critical for promoting sustainability and protecting the health of communities. By working together with our communities to identify and address these issues, we can create a healthier and more sustainable future for ourselves and for future generations.

6.2 STARTING YOUR LOCAL ENVIRONMENTAL ASSESSMENT

As a budding environmental leader, conducting a local environmental assessment is a chance to show off your knowledge, identify issues that are actively impacting your community, and take steps to resolve them. But what exactly is a local environmental assessment, and how do you conduct one?

A local environmental assessment is a process of gathering information about environmental conditions in a specific geographic area. The information obtained is used to identify potential environmental risks and concerns and develop strategies to mitigate them.

The following are some of the steps involved in conducting a local environmental assessment:

6.2.1 Defining the study area and scope

To begin, determine the boundaries of the area to be assessed and the scope of the assessment. This can include factors such as the size of the area, the types of environmental issues to be assessed, and the resources available. You don't have to get fancy here. If it's a neighborhood problem, the boundaries are probably your neighborhood.

6.2.2 Identifying potential environmental issues and concerns

Once the study area and scope have been defined, it's important to identify potential environmental issues and concerns in the area. This can involve reviewing local regulations, gathering community input, and conducting site visits. It means talking to your neighbors about what's going on and seeing if they're concerned, too.

6.2.3 Collecting baseline data on environmental conditions and trends

With potential environmental issues identified, the next step is to collect baseline data on environmental conditions and trends. This can include data related to air and water quality, land use and zoning, demographic and socioeconomic factors, and climate and weather patterns. You can find existing data, ask for help from your local government or nonprofit, or find a University professor willing to help.

6.2.4 Analyzing the data to identify patterns and trends

After the data has been collected, it's important to analyze it to identify patterns and trends. This can help to pinpoint specific environmental issues that need to be addressed, and inform the development of strategies to mitigate them. It's fine if you don't have formal statistics training. What matters more is the storytelling: so focus on peak values, stories from community members, and data that tell the whole picture.

6.3 COLLECTING AND ANALYZING DATA

After defining the scope of a local environmental assessment and identifying potential environmental issues and concerns, the next step is to collect data related to those issues. There are several types of data that can be collected as part of a local environmental assessment, including:

6.3.1 Air and water quality data

This includes data related to pollutants in the air and water, such as particulate matter, ozone, and bacteria. This data can be collected from local monitoring stations or through fieldwork, such as taking water samples from local streams or rivers.

6.3.2 Land use and zoning information

This includes data related to how land in the area is being used, such as residential, commercial, or industrial. This data can be obtained through local planning and zoning offices. Many counties now house this data online and it is freely accessible to the public.

6.3.3   Demographic and socioeconomic data

This includes data related to population characteristics, such as age, income, education level, and race. This data can be obtained from local government agencies or through surveys of local residents.

6.3.4   Survey data about the issue

Ask your neighbors about their perceptions of the problem and ask them to propose solutions, too. You can create an informal survey, or just talk to people and take great notes. You could also consider holding a community meeting in a free public space. Let folks know that you want to publicize what you find out.

6.3.5   Climate and weather data

This includes data related to temperature, precipitation, and other weather patterns in the area. This data can be obtained from local weather stations or through analysis of historical climate data.

To collect and analyze this data, it's important to identify reliable sources of data and use appropriate methods for collecting and analyzing the data. This can involve conducting fieldwork, such as taking water samples or conducting surveys of local residents.

6.4 STAKEHOLDER ENGAGEMENT

While collecting data is important for understanding the environmental conditions in a specific geographic area, it's equally important to engage with stakeholders in the community. This includes community members, local government officials, and environmental groups. Stakeholders is just a fancy academic word for "people who care about or who are affected by the problem." Don't overcomplicate it. Talk to your neighbors.

Engaging with stakeholders helps to build trust and increase local support for environmental initiatives. By involving community members in the process of identifying and addressing environmental issues, you can ensure that their concerns and priorities are addressed. Additionally, engaging with local government officials and environmental groups can help to identify potential partners and resources for addressing environmental issues.

There are several methods for engaging with stakeholders, including:

6.4.1 Hosting public meetings and forums

Public meetings and forums provide an opportunity for community members to learn about environmental issues and share their thoughts and concerns. These meetings can be hosted both in-person and virtually, depending on the needs and preferences of the community.

6.4.2 Conducting interviews or surveys

Conducting interviews or surveys with community members can provide valuable insights into local environmental concerns and priorities. These methods can be particularly useful for engaging with community members who may not attend public meetings or forums.

6.4.3 Establishing advisory committees or working groups

Establishing advisory committees or working groups can be an effective way to involve stakeholders in the decision-making process. These groups can include representatives from different sectors of the community and can help to ensure that diverse perspectives are represented in the decision-making process.

Overall, stakeholder engagement is a critical part of a local environmental assessment. By engaging with stakeholders in the community, budding environmental leaders can build trust, increase local support for environmental initiatives, and ensure that the concerns and priorities of the community are addressed.

6.5 COMMUNICATING EFFECTIVELY WITH DIFFERENT AUDIENCES

Effective communication is key to successfully addressing environmental issues in your community. However, not all audiences are the same, and it's important to tailor your communication strategies to specific audiences. Here are some tips for communicating effectively with different audiences:

6.5.1 Identifying target audiences

Before developing communication strategies, it's important to identify your target audiences. This can include community members, local government officials, business owners, media outlets, and other stakeholders. Each audience may have different concerns, priorities, and communication preferences.

6.5.2   Tailoring communication strategies to specific audiences

Once you have identified your target audiences, it's important to tailor your communication strategies to their specific needs. For example, community members may respond well to social media campaigns and public meetings, while local government officials may prefer formal presentations and reports.

6.5.3   Best practices for effective communication

Regardless of the audience, there are some best practices for effective communication. This includes keeping messages clear and concise, using visuals and other creative elements to convey information, and providing evidence to support your claims. It's also important to be transparent and honest in your communication, even if it means acknowledging challenges or limitations.

6.5.4   The call to action

Finally, it's important to provide a clear call to action for each audience. This could include asking community members to attend a public meeting, requesting a policy change from local government officials, or asking business owners to implement sustainable practices. The call to action should be specific, actionable, and tied to the overall goals of the project.

6.5.5   Case study: Communicating with people in power

When it comes to addressing environmental issues, it's important to communicate effectively with people in positions of power, such as politicians and government officials. These individuals have the ability to make significant changes that can impact the health and sustainability of your community. Here are some tips for communicating effectively in this context:

1. Be professional: When communicating with people in power, it's important to present yourself in a professional manner. This means dressing appropriately, using proper language and tone, and being respectful even if there are disagreements.

2. Be prepared: Before your meeting or presentation, make sure you have done your research and are prepared to answer questions and provide evidence to support your claims. Anticipate potential objections and have responses ready.

3. Use clear and concise language: When presenting your ideas, use clear and concise language to convey your message. Avoid jargon or technical terms that may be unfamiliar to your audience.

4. Focus on the most important points: People in power are often busy and may have limited time to dedicate to your issue. Focus on the most important points and be clear about what action you are asking them to take.

5. Make a strong case: Use data and evidence to support your case, including information about the potential benefits of taking action and the risks of not doing so.

6. Follow up: After your meeting or presentation, follow up with the people in power to thank them for their time and reiterate your message. This can help keep your issue top of mind and increase the likelihood of action being taken.

    Overall, communicating effectively with people in power requires preparation, professionalism, and a strong case supported by evidence. By following these tips, you can increase the likelihood that your message will be heard and acted upon, leading to positive change for your community.

6.5.6 Other tips for communicating effectively

Communicating effectively with different audiences is a critical part of addressing environmental issues in your community. By identifying target audiences, tailoring communication strategies, using best practices for effective communication, and providing a clear call to action, you can increase the likelihood that your message will be heard and acted upon.

6.6 DEVELOPING A PRIORITIZATION PLAN OR REPORT

After identifying potential environmental issues and engaging with stakeholders in the community, the next step is to develop a prioritization plan or report. This involves setting criteria for prioritization, evaluating potential solutions based on their effectiveness, feasibility, and cost, and selecting the most appropriate solutions and developing an action plan.

Setting criteria for prioritization involves identifying the factors that are most important for addressing environmental issues in the community. This can include factors such as the severity and urgency of the issue, the potential impact on human health and the environment, and the availability of resources and funding.

Once criteria have been set, potential solutions can be evaluated based on their effectiveness, feasibility, and cost. Effective solutions should be backed by evidence and have a clear pathway to achieving the desired outcome. Feasible solutions should be practical and able to be implemented within the available timeframe and resources. Cost-effective solutions should provide a good return on investment and be affordable within the available budget.

After evaluating potential solutions, the most appropriate solutions can be selected and an action plan can be developed. The action plan should outline the steps needed to implement the chosen solutions, including timelines, budgets, and responsibilities.

It's important to remember that the development of a prioritization plan or report is not a one-time event. Ongoing monitoring and evaluation is critical for tracking progress and adjusting the plan as needed. This can involve regular reporting on progress, collecting feedback from stakeholders, and revising the plan as new information becomes available.

6.6.1 Case study: Presenting Your Plan To People With Power

As an environmental leader, you may find yourself in situations where you've done all the work of identifying environmental issues, conducting assessments, and developing a prioritization plan, but you're still struggling to get the attention of the people who have the power to make change. In these situations, organizing tactics can be useful.

Protests, rallies, sit-ins, and other forms of direct action can be effective in bringing attention to environmental issues and putting pressure on decision-makers to take action. However, it's important to remember that direct action is just one tool in the toolbox. It's important to seek out collaborative options and have concrete asks when engaging with decision-makers.

For example, instead of staging a protest, you could ask for a meeting with the decision-maker to present your plan and discuss potential solutions. Alternatively, you could ask for a letter of support or a public hearing to raise awareness of the issue and gather feedback from the community.

It's important to approach these interactions with decision-makers in a professional and respectful manner. Be prepared to answer questions and provide evidence to support your plan. Remember that decision-makers are often busy and may not have much time to dedicate to the issue, so be concise and clear in your presentation.

6.6.2 Keeping The People Motivated

As an environmental leader, getting people motivated and involved in your project is key to creating positive change in your community. However, as time goes on, it can be difficult to maintain that momentum and keep people engaged. Here are some tips for keeping the people motivated:

6.6.3 Involve people every step of the way

Make sure to involve people in every aspect of your project, from identifying environmental issues to implementing solutions. This helps people feel invested in the project and gives them a sense of ownership.

6.6.4 Communicate regularly

Keep people informed about the progress of the project and the impact it's having on the community. Use social media, email newsletters, and other communication tools to keep people engaged and up-to-date.

6.6.5 Recognize and celebrate successes

Celebrate the accomplishments of the project and recognize the hard work and dedication of the people involved. This helps to build morale and keep people motivated.

6.6.6 Provide opportunities for learning and growth

Offer training sessions, workshops, and other educational opportunities to help people develop new skills and knowledge related to environmental issues.

6.6.7 Foster a sense of community

Create opportunities for people to connect with each other and build relationships based on their shared interests in environmental issues. This helps to create a sense of community and support for the project.

Overall, keeping people motivated is a critical part of creating positive change in your community. By involving people every step of the way, communicating regularly, recognizing successes, providing opportunities for learning and growth, and fostering a sense of community, you can keep people engaged and committed to making a difference

6.7 CASE STUDIES OF ENVIRONMENTAL ISSUES AND SOLUTIONS

In addition to the steps involved in conducting a local environmental assessment, it's important to look at real-world examples of environmental issues and solutions. Here are three case studies that illustrate some of the challenges and opportunities for promoting sustainability and protecting the environment:

6.7.1   Case Study 1: Urban Air Quality

Urban air quality is a significant environmental issue that affects millions of people worldwide. In many urban areas, air pollution is caused by a variety of sources, including transportation, industrial activities, and energy generation.

To address this issue, many cities have implemented measures to reduce air pollution, such as promoting public transportation, encouraging the use of electric vehicles, and implementing regulations on industrial emissions. Additionally, some cities have implemented green infrastructure projects such as planting trees and creating green spaces to help improve air quality.

6.7.2   Case Study 2: Plastic Pollution in Oceans

Plastic pollution in oceans is a major environmental issue that threatens aquatic life and ecosystems. Plastic waste is often discarded into oceans, where it can harm marine animals and contribute to the formation of large oceanic garbage patches.

To address this issue, many countries have implemented regulations on single-use plastics such as straws, bags, and utensils. Additionally, some organizations have implemented ocean cleanup efforts that involve collecting plastic waste from oceans. Another solution to this problem is promoting recycling and the use of biodegradable materials in place of plastics.

6.7.3 Case Study 3: Sustainable Agriculture in Local Communities

Sustainable agriculture is an important issue that involves balancing the needs of food production with environmental sustainability. In many local communities, sustainable agriculture practices are being implemented to promote healthy soil and water management, reduce pesticide use, and increase yields.

Some sustainable agriculture practices include regenerative agriculture, which involves using natural processes to build soil health, crop rotation, and intercropping. By implementing these practices, local communities can achieve sustainable food production that benefits both the environment and local economies.

Overall, these case studies illustrate the challenges and opportunities for promoting sustainability and protecting the environment. By learning from these examples and implementing best practices in our own communities, we can work towards creating a healthier, more sustainable future.

6.8 CONCLUSION

In this chapter, we explored the importance of identifying local environmental issues and the steps involved in conducting a local environmental assessment. We discussed the different types of data that can be collected as part of an assessment, methods for engaging with stakeholders, and how to develop a prioritization plan or report for addressing identified environmental issues.

As budding environmental leaders, it's important to apply the knowledge and strategies presented in this chapter to our own communities. By conducting a local environmental assessment, engaging with stakeholders, and developing a prioritization plan or report, we can work towards creating positive change in our communities.

We encourage readers to take action and apply the knowledge gained from this chapter to identify and address local environmental issues. By doing so, we can promote sustainability and protect the health of our communities, making a positive impact on both present and future generations.

6.9 Reflection Questions

1. How can identifying local environmental issues and conducting environmental assessments benefit both the environment and the health of your community?

2. What are some of the challenges involved in conducting a local environmental assessment, and how can you overcome these challenges?

3. How can you engage with stakeholders in a way that promotes collaboration and constructive dialogue?

4. What are some of the different types of data that can be collected as part of a local environmental assessment, and how can this data be used to inform decision-making?

5. Why is it important to communicate effectively with different audiences when addressing environmental issues, and what are some strategies for tailoring communication to specific audiences?

6. What role do politicians and people in power play in addressing environmental issues, and how can you effectively communicate with them to advocate for change?

7. How can you keep people motivated and engaged in environmental projects over the long term?

8. How can you use organizing tactics such as protests, rallies, and sit-ins to draw attention to environmental issues and pressure decision-makers to take action?

9. What are some best practices for communicating clearly and effectively, and how can you apply these practices in your work?

10. How can you identify and prioritize environmental issues in your community, and what steps can you take to address these issues in a meaningful way?

6.10 SUGGESTED ACTIVITIES

1. Conduct a local environmental assessment of your community: You can start by identifying environmental issues that are affecting your community and conducting a detailed assessment of these issues. This could include gathering data on air and water quality, identifying potential sources of pollution, and assessing the impact of climate change on your community.

2. Organize a public meeting or rally: You can use organizing tactics such as public meetings or rallies to draw attention to environmental issues and pressure decision-makers to take action. This can involve inviting community members, local government officials, and other stakeholders to discuss the issue and work towards solutions.

3. Develop a communication plan for addressing an environmental issue: You can create a communication plan that outlines how you will communicate with different

audiences, such as community members, politicians, and business owners, about an environmental issue. This could include developing a social media campaign, creating informational materials like flyers or brochures, and setting up meetings or presentations to discuss the issue.

---

7 EXPANDING YOUR KNOWLEDGE

As environmental leaders, it is essential to stay informed and continue expanding your knowledge about environmental issues and solutions. However, learning doesn't have to involve going back to school or earning another degree. There are plenty of alternative learning opportunities available, from online courses and webinars to hands-on experiences and specialized knowledge in a specific area of interest.

Expanding your environmental knowledge also involves building a network of environmental professionals and advocates, participating in community and professional organizations, and sharing your knowledge and experiences with others. In this chapter, we'll explore these topics and provide strategies for staying informed, building your network, sharing knowledge, and continuing to develop your environmental knowledge.

7.1 STAYING INFORMED AND UPDATED

Staying informed about environmental issues is essential for anyone who wants to make a positive change in their community. With so much information available, it can be challenging to know where to look. Here are some resources that can help you stay up-to-date and informed about the latest environmental issues:

7.1.1 News Outlets

The New York Times, National Geographic, Environmental Health News, and The Guardian are all reputable news sources that cover environmental issues on a regular basis. These publications provide in-depth reporting on environmental issues and are great resources for keeping up with new developments.

Your library may provide free access to many, if not all of these resources. You can ask your librarian about the Libby app for books and magazines, or an app like Press Reader for the news. They may also offer direct access to specific publications: my library offers the NY Times for free.

7.1.2 Podcasts

Green Dreamer, Living on Earth, and The Energy Gang are just a few podcasts that focus on environmental issues. Podcasts can be an excellent way to stay informed while you're on-the-go, and they often feature interviews with experts in the field. Just keep an eye on dates, as sometimes podcasts will stop posting new episodes.

7.1.3 Online Forums

Reddit's r/Environmentalism and r/Sustainability are both online forums dedicated to discussing environmental issues. These forums can be a great place to connect with like-minded people and learn more about specific topics.

7.1.4 Social Media

Following reputable environmental organizations, experts, and advocates on social media platforms like Twitter and LinkedIn can be a great way to stay informed about the latest developments in the field.

7.1.5   Newsletters

Many environmental organizations offer newsletters that provide updates on their work and the latest developments in the field. This could be a great way to stay updated on specific issues that you care about.

7.2   STRATEGIES FOR FILTERING INFORMATION

With so much information available, it can be challenging to filter out what's relevant and reliable. To help sift through the noise, consider using filters like those offered by Google Alerts to receive updates on specific topics or areas of interest. Another strategy is to follow reputable sources and experts on social media platforms like Twitter or LinkedIn.

In today's world, we have access to an overwhelming amount of information, and it can be challenging to filter out what's relevant and reliable. To stay informed about environmental issues, it's essential to develop strategies for filtering information effectively. Here are some tips:

7.2.1   Use Filters

Google Alerts is a powerful tool that allows you to receive email updates about specific topics or areas of interest. By setting up alerts for environmental keywords or phrases, you can receive regular updates about the latest news and developments in your area of interest.

7.2.2 Follow Reputable Sources and Experts

Following reputable sources and experts on social media platforms like Twitter and LinkedIn can be a great way to stay informed about the latest developments in the field. By following individuals who are respected in the environmental community, you'll see more trustworthy and reliable information.

7.2.3 Check Sources and Citations

When reading articles or publications, be sure to check the sources and citations used by the authors. Reputable sources usually provide evidence to support their claims, so be wary of publications that lack sources or use dubious ones.

7.2.4 Look for Consensus

When looking at different perspectives on an issue, try to identify where there is consensus among experts. This can help you determine what information is most reliable and what claims are supported by the largest body of evidence.

7.2.5 Be Critical

Finally, it's important to be critical of the information you consume. Ask questions, fact-check claims, and look for multiple sources before drawing conclusions. This doesn't mean that all media is bad or "fake news" - just that the internet has democratized information. And the internet is NOT always right.

7.3 Connecting with Experts and Mentors

As an environmental leader, it's important to build a network of professionals and advocates who can support you in your work. Connecting with experts and mentors is one great way to expand your environmental knowledge and stay informed about the latest developments in the field. Here are some strategies for building your network:

7.3.1 Attend Conferences and Events

Attending conferences and events is a great way to connect with other environmental leaders, learn about new developments in the field, and gain inspiration for your work. Be sure to attend events that are relevant to your area of interest, and take advantage of opportunities to network with other attendees.

7.3.2 Reach out to Professionals

Don't be afraid to reach out to professionals in your area of interest. You can do this by sending an email, making a phone call, or connecting with them on LinkedIn. Many professionals are happy to share their knowledge and expertise with others, and they may be able to provide you with valuable guidance and advice.

7.3.3 Join Professional Organizations

Joining a professional organization is another great way to connect with other environmental leaders and stay informed about the latest developments in the field. These organizations often offer networking opportunities, training programs, and other resources that can help you build your skills and knowledge.

7.3.4 Participate in Mentorship Programs

Many organizations offer mentorship programs that can connect you with experienced professionals in your area of interest. These programs can provide you with guidance, support, and advice as you navigate your career in the environmental field.

7.3.5 Volunteer or Intern

Volunteering or interning with an environmental organization is another great way to build your network and gain hands-on experience. By working alongside experienced professionals, you'll have the opportunity to learn from them and develop your skills and knowledge.

7.4 YOU DON'T NEED TO GO BACK TO SCHOOL TO BECOME AN EXPERT

Many people believe that becoming an expert in any field requires going back to school and earning another degree. However, this is not always the case – there are many alternative learning opportunities available that can help you expand your knowledge and skills in the environmental field. Here are some ways you can develop your expertise without going back to school:

7.4.1 Alternative Learning Opportunities

Alternative learning opportunities are a great way to expand your environmental knowledge without the need to go back to school. Online courses, webinars, and workshops offer flexible and accessible learning options that can fit into any schedule.

Online platforms like Coursera, Udemy, and EdX offer a wide range of courses on environmental topics, ranging from introductory courses on environmental science to more specialized courses on conservation, sustainability, and renewable energy. These courses are often taught by experts in the field and can be completed at your own pace from anywhere in the world. They also provide an opportunity to interact with other students and professionals in discussion forums, allowing you to expand your network and learn from others.

In addition to online courses, many environmental organizations offer webinars and workshops on specific issues or topics. For example, the World Wildlife Fund offers webinars on various environmental topics, including conservation planning and sustainable finance. These webinars provide valuable insights and information from professionals who are working in the field.

7.4.2   Importance of Hands-On Experience

Hands-on experience is an essential part of expanding your environmental knowledge. While knowledge gained through books and online courses is valuable, hands-on experience can provide you with real-world insights and skills that cannot be learned through reading alone.

Volunteering with environmental organizations is a great way to gain hands-on experience in the field. Many organizations are always in need of volunteers to help with tasks like habitat restoration, wildlife monitoring, and public outreach. By volunteering, you can gain valuable experience in a specific area of interest, while also making a positive impact on the environment.

Participating in citizen science projects is another way to gain hands-on experience while contributing to scientific research. Citizen science projects allow individuals to collect data for scientific research by observing and recording information on environmental phenomena like bird populations, weather patterns, or water quality. By participating in a citizen science project, you can gain valuable experience in scientific research methods, while also contributing to important environmental research.

Interning with an environmental agency or NGO is another way to gain hands-on experience in the environmental field. Many organizations offer internships to students or recent graduates who are interested in gaining experience in a specific area of environmental work. These internships can provide valuable experience in areas like policy development, conservation planning, or environmental education.

7.4.3 Developing Specialized Knowledge in a Specific Area of Interest

Developing specialized knowledge in a specific area of interest is a great way to expand your environmental knowledge and become an expert in a particular aspect of environmental work. By focusing your attention on one area, you can gain a deeper understanding of the issue and become a valuable resource for others who are interested in that area.

There are many areas of environmental work where you can develop specialized knowledge, depending on your interests and career goals. For example, if you're interested in renewable energy, you could focus on solar or wind power and become an expert in that area. Alternatively, if you're interested in conservation, you could focus on a specific species or habitat type and become a conservation expert in that area.

There are many ways to develop specialized knowledge in a specific area of interest. Online courses, webinars, and workshops can provide specialized knowledge on a variety of topics, while conferences and events can provide valuable networking opportunities with other professionals in the field. Additionally, volunteering with environmental organizations or participating in citizen science projects can provide hands-on experience in a specific area of interest.

Developing specialized knowledge in a specific area of interest can also help you stand out in a crowded field of environmental professionals. By becoming an expert in a specific area, you can position yourself as a go-to resource for others who are looking for information or advice on that topic.

7.5 WHO YOU KNOW IS AS IMPORTANT AS WHAT YOU KNOW

In the environmental field, who you know can be just as important as what you know. Building a strong network of environmental professionals and advocates can open up new opportunities, provide support and guidance, and help you stay informed about the latest developments in the field. Here are some strategies for building your network:

7.5.1 Strategies for Building a Network

Building a network of environmental professionals and advocates is an essential part of expanding your environmental knowledge and career opportunities. There are many strategies for building your network, including:

1. **Attending Conferences and Events:** Attending conferences and events focused on environmental issues is a great way to meet other professionals in the field and build relationships with like-minded individuals. These events provide valuable opportunities to network, attend informative sessions, and learn about new developments in the field.

2. **Joining Online Communities and Forums:** Joining online communities or forums focused on environmental issues provides another opportunity to connect with other professionals and advocates in the field. These communities can be found on platforms like LinkedIn, Reddit, or Facebook, and provide a space for discussion, information sharing, and collaboration.

3. **Participating in Online Discussions:** Participating in online discussions related to environmental issues is a great way to engage with other professionals and advocates in the field. This can include commenting on blog posts, tweeting using relevant hashtags, or participating in discussion forums.

4. **Engaging with Other Environmental Leaders on Social Media:** Social media platforms like LinkedIn, Twitter, and Instagram can also be powerful tools for building your network. By following and engaging with other environmental leaders and organizations on these platforms, you can stay up-to-date on the latest trends and developments in the field, and potentially make valuable connections.

   Overall, building a network of environmental professionals and advocates is essential for anyone looking to expand their environmental knowledge and career opportunities. By attending conferences and events, joining online communities, participating in online discussions, and engaging with other environmental leaders on social media, you can build meaningful relationships and develop your expertise in the field.

7.5.2 Importance of Mentorship and Collaboration

Mentorship and collaboration are important aspects of building your network and expanding your environmental knowledge. By working with experienced professionals and collaborating with other environmental leaders, you can gain valuable insights, feedback, and guidance that can help you grow professionally.

Mentorship is a particularly valuable opportunity for anyone looking to expand their environmental knowledge. A mentor is someone who has experience in the field and can provide guidance, advice, and support to help you achieve your career goals. Mentors can provide feedback on your work, offer suggestions for new opportunities, and share their own experiences and insights.

Collaboration is another valuable strategy for building your network and expanding your environmental knowledge. Working collaboratively with other environmental leaders provides an opportunity to learn new skills, share experiences, and build relationships with others in the field. Collaborative projects can take many forms, from research projects to community-based initiatives, and can provide valuable opportunities for professional growth and learning.

Overall, mentorship and collaboration are important strategies for anyone looking to build their network and expand their environmental knowledge. By working closely with experienced professionals and collaborating with other environmental leaders, you can gain valuable insights, feedback, and guidance that can help you grow professionally while also contributing to positive environmental outcomes.

7.5.3 Participating in Community and Professional Organizations

Partating in community and professional organizations is a great way to build your network of environmental professionals and advocates. Community organizations such as local conservation groups and neighborhood associations provide opportunities to participate in grassroots environmental initiatives, volunteer for environmental causes, and connect with like-minded individuals.

Professional organizations are another option, such as the National Wildlife Federation or the Sierra Club, which provide valuable networking opportunities with other environmental professionals. These organizations often hold conferences, workshops, and other events that allow members to share ideas, learn from experts in the field, and connect with other professionals.

Participation in these organizations can also be a great way to build your skills and knowledge about specific aspects of environmental work. Many organizations offer training programs, mentorship opportunities, or leadership roles that provide valuable experience in areas such as conservation, sustainability, or policy development.

Overall, participating in community and professional organizations can be a valuable strategy for anyone looking to expand their environmental knowledge and build their network of environmental professionals and advocates. These organizations provide opportunities to connect with others who share your passion for environmental issues, participate in collaborative projects, and attend events and conferences that can help you grow professionally.

7.6 Don't Hoard Knowledge, Share It All

As an environmental professional or advocate, it's important to remember that knowledge is power, and sharing knowledge can have a transformative impact on your work. By sharing your experiences, expertise, and insights with others, you can help to build a community of environmental leaders who are well-informed, inspired, and motivated to make a positive impact. Here are some reasons why sharing knowledge is so critical in the environmental field:

7.6.1 Benefits of Sharing Knowledge and Experiences

Sharing knowledge and experiences is an essential part of building a community of environmental leaders who are informed, inspired, and motivated to make a positive impact. By sharing your knowledge and experiences, you can inspire others to take action, build new relationships, and advance the field as a whole.

One of the main benefits of sharing knowledge and experiences is the development of new ideas. When professionals share their knowledge and experiences, they can discover new approaches and solutions to environmental challenges. Collaborations and partnerships can also develop from these exchanges, leading to the development of innovative solutions that benefit both the environment and society.

Sharing knowledge and experiences also encourages the sharing of best practices. As environmental leaders exchange knowledge, they are more likely to adopt best practices in their work, leading to greater efficiency and effectiveness in addressing environmental challenges. This can lead to better outcomes for the environment and, ultimately, society as a whole.

Another benefit of sharing knowledge and experiences is the building of relationships with other professionals and advocates. Sharing knowledge can lead to new opportunities for collaborations, partnerships, and joint initiatives, which can increase the impact of environmental efforts and create more sustainable outcomes.

Overall, sharing knowledge and experiences is critical to building a community of environmental leaders who are informed, inspired, and motivated to make a positive impact. The benefits of this exchange include the development of new ideas, the sharing of best practices, and the building of relationships that can lead to new opportunities, collaborations, and partnerships.

7.6.2 Building a Personal Brand as an Environmental Expert

Building a personal brand as an environmental expert and advocate is a great way to stand out in a crowded field and attract new clients or collaborators. By sharing your knowledge and experiences, you can position yourself as a leader in the environmental community and inspire others to take action. To build your personal brand, there are several strategies you can consider:

1. **Create a Website or Blog**: Creating a website or blog focused on environmental issues is a great way to share your thoughts and insights with a wider audience. This can help you build a

following and establish yourself as a thought leader in the field.

2. **Participate in Online Discussions**: Participating in online discussions related to environmental issues is a great way to showcase your expertise and engage with other professionals and advocates. This can include commenting on blog posts, tweeting using relevant hashtags, or participating in discussion forums.

3. **Use Social Media Platforms**: Social media platforms like LinkedIn, Twitter, and Instagram can also be powerful tools for building your personal brand. By sharing your thoughts and insights on environmental issues, you can attract followers and connect with other professionals in the field.

4. **Speak at Conferences and Events**: Speaking at conferences and events provides an opportunity to showcase your expertise and position yourself as a leader in the field. This can help you attract new clients or collaborators and increase your visibility among other environmental professionals.

5. **Write Articles or Reports**: Writing articles or reports on environmental issues allows you to showcase your expertise and position yourself as a thought leader in the field. These articles can be published in journals, magazines, or online platforms, providing an opportunity to reach a broader range of readers and establish yourself as a go-to resource for others in the field.

> Building a personal brand as an environmental expert and advocate can help you stand out in a competitive field and attract new clients or collaborators. Sharing knowledge and experiences is a critical part of success in the environmental field.

1. What are some new resources for staying informed about environmental issues that you learned about in this chapter?

2. How can you apply the strategies for filtering information effectively to your own work?

3. Who are some environmental professionals or advocates that you could reach out to for mentorship or advice?

4. What are some alternative learning opportunities that you could take advantage of to develop your environmental knowledge?

5. How can building a network of environmental professionals and advocates benefit your work in the field?

6. What are some community or professional organizations that you could join to expand your network and build relationships with other environmental leaders?

7. How can sharing your knowledge and experiences with others help you build a personal brand as an environmental expert?

8. What are some specific areas of environmental work that you would like to develop specialized knowledge in?

9. How can you apply the strategies for connecting with experts and mentors to your own career development goals?

10. What steps will you take to continue developing your environmental knowledge and skills after reading this chapter?

7.8 SUGGESTED ACTIVITIES

1. Attend an Environmental Conference or Event - Attending a conference or event focused on environmental issues is a great way to expand your knowledge and build connections with other environmental leaders. Research upcoming conferences or events in your area of interest, and make plans to attend one that aligns with your goals. While you're there, be sure to take advantage of

networking opportunities, attend sessions that align with your interests, and engage with other attendees.

2. Join an Online Course or Webinar - Online courses and webinars are accessible, affordable ways to gain specialized knowledge in a specific area of interest. Research online platforms like Coursera, Udemy, or EdX, or look for webinars offered by environmental organizations or agencies. Choose a topic that aligns with your interests or professional development goals, and commit to completing the course or attending the webinar.

3. Start a blog or vlog about your environmental work - Starting a blog or vlog about your environmental work is a great way to share your experiences and insights with others, while also building your personal brand as an environmental expert. Choose a platform like WordPress or YouTube, and start creating content that highlights your work and experience. Be sure to promote your blog or vlog on social media and other online communities, and engage with other bloggers or vloggers to build your network.

8 EMBODYING ENVIRONMENTAL VALUES

Environmental leadership is about more than just taking action to protect the planet. It's about embodying a set of core values that underpin your work, guiding your decisions, and shaping your perspective on environmental issues. Environmental leaders who embody these values are more likely to be effective in their work, build strong relationships with other professionals and advocates, and inspire others to take action.

8.1 CORE VALUES OF ENVIRONMENTAL LEADERSHIP

So, what are the core values that underpin environmental leadership? There are several key values that are essential for effective environmental leadership, including ethics, empathy, responsibility, and resilience.

8.1.1 Ethics

Ethics are a fundamental part of environmental leadership. Acting in an ethical manner means taking responsibility for the impacts of your work, being honest and transparent in your communication, and treating all living beings with respect and dignity. Environmental leaders who prioritize ethical behavior are more likely to build trust with others in the field and gain credibility as effective advocates for the planet.

Ethics is a fundamental value that underpins environmental leadership. Acting in an ethical manner means taking responsibility for the impacts of your work, being honest and transparent in your communication, and treating all living beings with respect and dignity. As an environmental leader, it is essential to prioritize ethics in your work to ensure that your actions align with your values and beliefs.

So, what does it mean to act in an ethical manner as an environmental leader? First and foremost, it means taking responsibility for the impacts of your work on the environment and society. Ethical environmental leaders recognize the interconnectedness of all living beings and understand that their actions can have far-reaching consequences. This means that sometimes we do things that have a different impact than what we intended. Taking ownership of our failures, and understanding that impact is more important than intent, is an important ethical practice.

Another essential element of ethical environmental leadership is honesty and transparency. Environmental leaders who prioritize ethics are open and transparent in their communication, sharing accurate and timely information about environmental issues and the impacts of their work. By being transparent, they can build trust with others in the field and demonstrate their commitment to environmental protection. However, being transparent does not mean gossip or violating perceived secrecy. For example, it is usually unethical to record and then share conversations without consent.

Treating all living beings with respect and dignity is another critical aspect of ethical environmental leadership. This includes humans as well as animals, plants, and ecosystems. Ethical environmental leaders prioritize the value of all life and take steps to protect and preserve biodiversity. They recognize that all living beings have inherent worth and seek to minimize harm in their actions. We can act ethically by avoiding ad-hominem attacks on people that we disagree with. Instead, we attack their reasoning, not their characters.

Ethics is a critical value for environmental leaders. To act in an ethical manner means taking responsibility for the impacts of your work, being honest and transparent in your communication, and treating all living beings with respect and dignity. By prioritizing ethics in your work, you can build trust with others in the field, demonstrate your commitment to environmental protection, and inspire others to follow your lead.

8.1.2   Empathy

Empathy is a fundamental value for effective environmental leadership. It is the ability to consider the needs of all living beings affected by environmental issues, including humans, animals, and ecosystems. By prioritizing empathy in their work, environmental leaders can better understand the complex interconnections between people and the environment and develop solutions that work for all stakeholders.

Empathy allows environmental leaders to see beyond their own perspectives and understand the perspectives of others. They can recognize the different needs and values of stakeholders who are involved in environmental issues, such as local communities, businesses, government agencies, and non-profit organizations. This understanding can help them develop solutions that address the needs of all stakeholders, rather than just a select few.

Environmental leaders who prioritize empathy also understand the impacts of environmental issues on human health, social justice, and economic stability. They recognize that marginalized communities are often disproportionately impacted by environmental problems, such as pollution, habitat loss, and climate change. By prioritizing empathy, they can advocate for effective solutions that are inclusive and equitable for all members of society.

Empathy does not mean infantilizing groups of people. Adults living in polluted communities are not infants in need of your assistance. They have voices, ideas, and even capital. Work with, and listen to people across your community.

Additionally, empathy allows environmental leaders to develop a deeper connection to nature and wildlife. They recognize the inherent value of all living beings and seek to protect and preserve biodiversity. Empathetic leaders understand that people are interconnected with the environment and that our actions have consequences for the natural world.

Empathy is a critical value for effective environmental leadership. By prioritizing empathy in their work, environmental leaders can better understand the needs of all stakeholders, develop solutions that address social and economic justice, and advocate for the protection and preservation of biodiversity.

8.1.3 Responsibility

Responsibility is a fundamental value for effective environmental leadership. It is the ability to acknowledge the impacts of our actions on the environment and take steps to mitigate those impacts. Environmental leaders who prioritize responsibility are committed to reducing their carbon footprint, conserving natural resources, and protecting wildlife and ecosystems.

Environmental leaders who prioritize responsibility recognize that their actions can have far-reaching consequences for the environment and society. They understand that their work has a significant impact on the natural world and seek to minimize harm in their decisions. This includes taking practical steps to reduce waste, conserve energy, and promote sustainable practices in all aspects of their work.

Additionally, responsible environmental leaders prioritize the protection and preservation of biodiversity. They recognize the importance of wildlife and ecosystems and understand that they are essential to the health and well-being of the planet. Through responsible actions, environmental leaders can help protect and restore habitats and species that are threatened by human activities.

Furthermore, responsible environmental leaders understand that they have a duty to future generations to act in a way that promotes sustainability. They recognize that our planet's resources are finite and must be managed in a way that ensures their availability for future generations.

Responsibility is a critical value for effective environmental leadership. By taking responsibility for their actions, environmental leaders can show others that environmental protection is not just about advocacy, but also about taking practical steps to address environmental challenges.

8.1.4   Resilience

Resilience is a critical value for effective environmental leadership. It is the ability to adapt and respond to changing environmental conditions, such as climate change, pollution, or habitat loss. By fostering resilience in ourselves and our communities, we can better weather environmental challenges and emerge stronger and more prepared to protect the planet.

Environmental leaders who prioritize resilience understand that environmental issues are complex and require innovative solutions. They recognize that the natural world is constantly evolving and that we must be prepared to adapt to these changes. By prioritizing resilience, environmental leaders can develop strategies that are flexible, responsive, and sustainable.

Additionally, resilient environmental leaders recognize that building resilience is not just about individual actions but also about building strong communities. They work together with other professionals and advocates to identify shared goals and develop collaborative solutions. Through building strong partnerships and networks, they can create resilient communities that can effectively respond to environmental challenges.

Furthermore, resilient environmental leaders understand that environmental issues affect different communities differently, and they prioritize environmental justice in their work. They recognize that marginalized communities often have fewer resources to adapt to environmental challenges and seek to promote equity and inclusion in all aspects of environmental protection.

Resilience is a critical value for effective environmental leadership. By fostering resilience in ourselves and our communities, we can better weather environmental challenges and emerge stronger and more prepared to protect the planet.

8.2 ALIGNING ACTIONS WITH BELIEFS AND PRINCIPLES

As an environmental leader, it is essential to align your actions with your beliefs and principles. When your actions are in line with your environmental values, you are more likely to inspire others to join you in your efforts to protect the planet. Aligning your actions with your beliefs and principles can also help you stay focused and motivated as you work towards your goals.

Here are some of the benefits of aligning your actions with your environmental values:

8.2.1 Increased credibility

When your actions are aligned with what you say, it becomes easier to gain the trust and respect of others. This is especially true in environmental leadership, where authenticity and integrity are essential for building relationships with stakeholders and inspiring action.

When you act in a way that aligns with your environmental values, you demonstrate to others that you are committed to protecting the planet. This consistency between your words and actions builds trust with others and enhances your credibility as an environmental leader. People are more likely to follow a leader who practices what they preach, rather than someone who says one thing but does another.

Aligning your actions with your environmental values can also help you build stronger relationships with stakeholders. It shows that you are invested in the same outcomes and fosters trust that you have similar values. This trust is crucial when working with partners, policymakers, and other stakeholders as it allows you to work closely together towards shared environmental goals.

In contrast, if your actions do not align with your values, it can be challenging to gain the trust of others. This inconsistency can lead to skepticism and even distrust, which can harm your ability to effectively lead and work with others towards environmental goals.

8.2.2 Improved decision-making

Improved decision-making is another significant benefit of aligning your actions with your beliefs and values. When you have a clear understanding of your core environmental values, you are better equipped to make decisions that align with those values.

Knowing your values can help you prioritize what is important to you, which can help guide your decision-making process. For example, if your core value is promoting sustainability, you may prioritize decisions that reduce waste, conserve resources, or protect biodiversity.

By making decisions that align with your values, you can avoid situations where you compromise your environmental principles. It can also help you identify opportunities where you can advocate for positive environmental change.

In contrast, if you do not have a clear understanding of your values, it can be challenging to make decisions that are consistent with your environmental principles. This can lead to decision-making that is inconsistent and may not lead to the outcomes that you desire.

Ultimately, improved decision-making helps you become more effective in your environmental leadership role. Making decisions that align with your values can help you stay focused on your environmental goals and make progress towards them. It can also help you identify opportunities for positive change and advocate for policies and practices that promote environmental protection.

8.2.3 Greater motivation

Greater motivation is another significant benefit of aligning your actions with your beliefs and values. When you are working towards something that you deeply believe in and care about, it can be motivating and satisfying.

By aligning your actions with your environmental values, you can create a sense of purpose and meaning in your work. This can help you stay committed to your environmental goals, even in the face of challenges or setbacks. Knowing that you are working towards something that is important to you can also give you a sense of fulfillment and achievement.

In contrast, if your actions do not align with your values, it can be challenging to find motivation and purpose in your work. This can lead to feelings of frustration or burnout, which can harm your ability to effectively lead and work towards environmental goals.

Moreover, aligning your actions with your values can help you inspire others to take action. People are more likely to be motivated by leaders who are passionate and committed to their cause. By being consistent and authentic in your actions, you can demonstrate your commitment to environmental protection and inspire others to join you in your efforts.

Ultimately, greater motivation helps you become a more effective environmental leader. By staying motivated and committed to your goals, you can inspire others, overcome challenges, and make progress towards environmental protection.

8.2.4 Identifying and clarifying your core environmental values

Identifying and clarifying your core environmental values is an essential step towards aligning your actions with your beliefs and principles.

Identifying your core values is crucial because it helps you understand what you stand for and what motivates you. When you have a clear understanding of your values, it becomes easier to make decisions that align with those values. It can also help you communicate your values to others and build stronger relationships.

There are several strategies for identifying and clarifying your core environmental values. Here are some additional points to consider:

1. Self-reflection and introspection: Take time to reflect on your personal beliefs and values. Ask yourself questions such as "What do I care about the most?" or "What motivates me to work towards environmental protection?"

2. Seeking feedback from peers and mentors: Seek input from people who know you well. They may be able to provide insight into your core values and how you can align your actions with them.

3. Conducting a values assessment: Many assessments are available online to help you identify your core values. These assessments can help you learn more about what you value most and how you can align your actions with those values.

8.2.4.1   *Examples of core environmental values*

Here are some additional examples of core environmental values:

1. Respect for all living beings: This value recognizes the inherent value and importance of all living beings. It includes animals, plants, and ecosystems. Actions that align with this value may include protecting habitats, promoting animal welfare, or advocating for biodiversity conservation.

2. Promoting sustainability: This value recognizes the need to protect the planet's resources for future generations. Actions

that align with this value may include reducing waste, conserving resources, or promoting sustainable practices.

3. Advocating for social and environmental justice: This value recognizes the interconnectedness of social and environmental issues. Actions that align with this value may include advocating for policies that promote environmental protection and social justice.

Identifying and clarifying your core environmental values is essential for effective environmental leadership. By using strategies such as self-reflection, seeking feedback, and conducting values assessments, you can gain a better understanding of what motivates you and how you can align your actions with your values. Examples of core environmental values such as respect for all living beings, promoting sustainability, and advocating for social and environmental justice can help guide your decision-making and actions towards positive environmental outcomes.

8.2.5 Aligning actions with your values

Aligning actions with your values is critical for leading an authentic and fulfilling life. It means being true to yourself and making decisions that align with your beliefs and principles. When you align your actions with your values, you are more likely to feel motivated, inspired, and fulfilled.

Furthermore, when it comes to environmental issues, aligning actions with values is essential for promoting sustainability and protecting the planet. By prioritizing actions that align with your environmental values, you can create a positive impact on the environment and inspire others to take action. Some strategies for aligning actions with values include: 1. **Setting clear goals and objectives:** Setting clear goals and objectives is crucial for aligning actions with values. Goals should be SMART - specific, measurable, achievable, relevant, and time-bound. By having clear goals, you can ensure that your actions are aligned with your values. For instance, if sustainability is one of your core values, you may set a goal to reduce your organization's carbon footprint by 50% by the end of the year. This goal helps you prioritize actions that align with your values, such as using renewable energy sources or reducing waste. 2. **Prioritizing actions that align with values:** Prioritizing actions that align with values is another strategy for aligning actions with values. Once you have identified your core values, you can prioritize actions that align with those values. For example, if biodiversity conservation is one of your core environmental values, you may prioritize actions that protect habitats, promote plant and animal diversity, or advocate for conservation policies. 3. **Integrating values into decision-making processes:** Integrating values into decision-making processes is essential for aligning actions with values. A framework that integrates values into decision-making processes can help you make more informed and ethical decisions that align with your values. For example, the triple bottom line approach is a framework that considers social, environmental, and economic factors when making decisions. This framework ensures that your actions align with your values, and it can help you make more sustainable decisions that benefit the planet and society.

8.2.5.1 *Examples of aligning actions with values*

1. **Implementing sustainable practices in daily operations:** Implementing sustainable practices in daily operations is an example of aligning actions with values. This can include using renewable energy sources, reducing waste, promoting recycling, and using eco-friendly products. These practices align with environmental values, such as promoting sustainability and protecting natural resources.

2. **Advocating for policies that promote environmental protection:** Advocating for policies that promote environmental protection is another example of aligning actions with values. This can include advocating for policies that protect natural habitats, reduce pollution, or promote renewable energy sources. These actions align with core environmental values, such as biodiversity conservation and sustainability.

3. **Incorporating environmental considerations into business practices:** Incorporating environmental considerations into business practices is an example of aligning actions with values. This can include assessing the environmental impact of products or services, reducing carbon footprint, or promoting environmentally friendly practices. These actions align with core environmental values and help promote sustainability.

Aligning your actions with your environmental values is crucial for effective environmental leadership. When your actions align with what you believe in, it becomes easier to gain the trust and respect of others. This consistency between your words and actions builds trust and enhances your credibility as an environmental leader. Moreover, aligning your actions with your values can help you make more informed decisions, stay motivated, and become a more effective advocate for environmental protection.

As environmental leaders, it is our responsibility to prioritize aligning our actions with our values. We must lead by example and demonstrate our commitment to environmental protection through our consistency, authenticity, and integrity. By prioritizing actions that align with our values, we can inspire others to join us in our efforts towards a sustainable future.

Environmental leaders have a critical role in promoting sustainability and protecting the planet. We must advocate for sustainable practices, promote awareness and education about environmental issues, and facilitate collaborations between stakeholders.

8.3 INSPIRING AND ENGAGING OTHERS TO EMBODY ENVIRONMENTAL VALUES

The environmental challenges facing the world today require collective action, and inspiring and engaging others to embody environmental values is essential for achieving sustainability goals. When people understand and embrace the importance of environmental values, they are more likely to make positive changes in their lives, take actions that protect the planet, and advocate for policies that promote environmental protection.

Effective communication is key to inspiring and engaging others to embody environmental values. Individuals and organizations need to have a clear understanding of their values and be able to communicate them effectively to their stakeholders. Strategies for communicating values effectively include using relatable language and stories, connecting with your audience on an emotional level, and providing actionable steps for people to take.

Another strategy for communicating values effectively is to lead by example. When people see others embodying environmental values through their actions, it can inspire them to take similar actions. By modeling environmentally responsible behavior, individuals and organizations can inspire and engage others to embody environmental values in their own lives.

In conclusion, inspiring and engaging others to embody environmental values is essential for achieving sustainability goals. Effective communication strategies, such as using relatable language and stories and leading by example, can help individuals and organizations communicate their values effectively and inspire others to take action.

8.3.1 Why is it important to inspire and engage others to embody environmental values?

Inspiring and engaging others to embody environmental values is critical for achieving sustainability goals and protecting the planet. There are several reasons why it is essential to inspire and engage others to care about environmental issues and to take action.

Firstly, inspiring and engaging others can increase awareness and interest in environmental issues. When more people are aware of environmental problems and understand their impact on the planet and society, they are more likely to take action to address these issues.

Secondly, inspiring and engaging others can encourage collective action and collaboration. By working together towards a common goal, we can achieve more than if we work alone. When people feel inspired and engaged, they are more likely to collaborate and take collective action to protect the environment.

Finally, inspiring and engaging others can foster a sense of community and shared purpose. When people are united by a common goal and share a sense of purpose, they are more likely to work together effectively and create lasting change. This sense of community can also provide support and motivation for individuals in their efforts to embody environmental values.

Inspiring and engaging others to embody environmental values is crucial for achieving sustainability goals. It can increase awareness and interest in environmental issues, encourage collective action and collaboration, and foster a sense of community and shared purpose.

8.3.2 Strategies for communicating your values effectively to others

Communicating your values effectively to others is essential for inspiring and engaging them to embody environmental values. There are several strategies that individuals and organizations can use to communicate their values effectively.

Firstly, it is essential to be clear and concise in your messaging. Your message should be easy to understand and articulate the value you want to communicate. Be sure to focus your message on the most important points and avoid using jargon or technical terms that could confuse your audience.

Secondly, using relatable language and stories can be an effective way to communicate your values. Use language that your audience can relate to and share stories that highlight the value and its importance. This approach can help create a personal connection and make your message more memorable.

Thirdly, connecting with your audience on an emotional level can be a powerful way to communicate your values. People are more likely to take action when they feel emotionally connected to an issue. Use language and stories that evoke emotions such as empathy, compassion, and inspiration to create an emotional connection with your audience.

Finally, providing actionable steps for people to take can make your message more compelling. People are more likely to take action when they have clear steps to follow. Provide practical steps that people can take to embody the value you are communicating, such as reducing their carbon footprint, supporting environmentally friendly policies, or volunteering for environmental organizations.

In conclusion, communicating your values effectively is essential for inspiring and engaging others to embody environmental values. Strategies such as being clear and concise in your messaging, using relatable language and stories, connecting with your audience on an emotional level, and providing actionable steps can help you communicate your values effectively.

8.4 CONCLUSION

Embodying environmental values is essential for effective environmental leadership. When leaders embody values such as sustainability, biodiversity conservation, and environmental protection, they can inspire and engage others to take action and create positive change. By aligning actions with values, leaders can create a more sustainable future for ourselves and future generations.

Furthermore, effective environmental leadership involves not just embodying environmental values, but also effectively communicating these values to others and inspiring them to take action. Leaders must use clear and concise messaging, relatable language and stories, emotional connection, and actionable steps to communicate their values effectively and engage others to embody environmental values.

In conclusion, embodying environmental values is a crucial aspect of effective environmental leadership. In aligning your actions with values and effectively communicating these values to others, you can inspire and engage others to embody environmental values and create a positive impact on the environment.

8.5 Reflective Questions

1. How well do I understand my own environmental values, and have I been able to align my actions with them?

2. What specific environmental values are important to me, and how can I better communicate them to others?

3. In what ways can I effectively inspire and engage others to embody environmental values?

4. Have I been able to effectively communicate the urgency of environmental issues to those around me?

5. How do I ensure that my personal and professional goals are aligned with my environmental values?

6. Have I taken action to promote sustainability in my local community, workplace, or industry?

7. In what ways can I collaborate with others who share similar environmental values to create positive change?

8. Have I considered the impacts of my daily choices and behaviors on the environment, and how can I make more environmentally friendly decisions?

9. In what ways have my experiences influenced my environmental values, and how have they evolved over time?

10. What steps can I take to continue learning about environmental issues and staying informed about current events related to sustainability?

8.6 Suggested Activities

1. Take some time to reflect on your environmental values and how well you have been embodying them. Write down a list of the values that are most important to you, and consider whether your actions align with these values. If there are areas where you feel you could do more, brainstorm some

specific actions you can take to better embody your environmental values.

2. Choose an environmental issue that you care about and research ways to take action. For example, if you are concerned about climate change, look into local or national policies that address this issue, consider reducing your carbon footprint, or find ways to support organizations that are working to combat climate change. Make a plan to take action, and share your ideas with friends and family to inspire them to do the same.

3. Connect with others who share your environmental values and collaborate on a project or initiative. Identify people in your community, workplace, or industry who are also passionate about sustainability and organize a meeting to discuss ideas for positive change. Consider working on a project together, such as implementing sustainable practices at work or organizing a community event to promote environmental awareness. Remember that working together can create a greater impact than working alone.

Environmental habits refer to the actions and behaviors we adopt in our daily lives that support the health and sustainability of our planet. Adopting sustainable habits, such as reducing waste, conserving energy, eating locally and seasonally, and using active transportation, are essential in achieving sustainable lifestyles. By cultivating these habits, we can reduce our environmental impact and preserve natural resources for future generations.

In this chapter, we will explore the concept of environmental habits and their importance in promoting environmental sustainability. We will provide an overview of the habits that support sustainable lifestyles and their contribution to environmental preservation. Additionally, we will discuss ways in which individuals can be responsible with the resources they have access to and how to incorporate sustainable habits into everyday life. We will also provide strategies for sharing and spreading these habits with others without coming off as pushy or judgmental.

Ultimately, this chapter aims to equip readers with the knowledge and tools needed to foster environmental habits in their own lives and communities. By adopting and promoting sustainable habits, we can collectively work towards a more sustainable and resilient future.

While identifying and improving our own habits is important, we must also keep in mind the reality of the situation. The climate crisis has been caused by a minority of oil and gas exploration companies. Learning to recycle may improve your life or your community, but it will not stop climate change. Even as we work to improve our own habits, we must not forget the corporate irresponsibility that got us here. But more on that in a later chapter.

9.1 Identifying Sustainable Habits

To identify sustainable habits, it is necessary to understand the habits that support sustainable lifestyles. These include:

9.1.1 Reducing waste

Reducing waste is a crucial aspect of adopting sustainable habits. The issue of waste has become a major environmental concern worldwide, as landfills continue to fill up and plastic pollution in oceans and waterways has reached staggering levels. By reducing waste through recycling, composting, and minimizing single-use plastics, individuals can significantly reduce their environmental impact.

Here in my county, I took a free composting class through our Parks system. In one of the classes, the waste management supervisor was invited to do a presentation. He said that up to 70% of what comes in via our waste channel - directly to the dump - could actually be composted or recycled instead. That really stuck with me. We could be diverting over 2/3rds of the volume of our dump with habit changes.

Recycling involves reusing materials instead of discarding them, which reduces the amount of waste that ends up in landfills. Recycling programs vary by location, but common items that can be recycled include paper, cardboard, glass, aluminum, and certain types of plastic. By recycling these materials, we can conserve natural resources, save energy and reduce greenhouse gas emissions.

Composting is another way of reducing waste. Composting involves taking organic waste materials such as food scraps, yard waste, and paper products and breaking them down into nutrient-rich soil. The resulting compost can then be used in gardens and farms as a natural fertilizer, reducing the need for chemical fertilizers. Composting also helps divert organic waste from landfills where it produces harmful methane gas.

Minimizing single-use plastics is perhaps one of the most important habits for reducing waste. Single-use plastics are items like straws, plastic bags, and cutlery that are used once and then discarded. These items are difficult to recycle and often end up in landfills or oceans, where they can harm wildlife and ecosystems. By switching to reusable bags, bottles, and containers, we can significantly reduce our plastic waste and our overall environmental impact.

[!attention] Accessibility Remember that waste can be an accessibility issue, too. Many rural areas may not offer recycling or even trash services. This is when community members resort to dumping or burning their trash. This requires systemic, town or county-level advocacy and change.

In conclusion, reducing waste through recycling, composting, and minimizing single-use plastics is an essential habit for achieving sustainable living. By adopting these habits, we can reduce our environmental footprint and contribute to a healthier planet.

9.1.2   Conserving energy

Conserving energy is another important habit for achieving sustainable living. The use of energy is closely tied to the production of greenhouse gases and climate change, making it critical that we conserve energy whenever possible. There are several ways to conserve energy in our daily lives, including:

1. Turning off lights and electronics when not in use: This may seem like a small habit, but it can significantly reduce energy usage. Lights and electronics left on when not in use waste energy and contribute to higher energy bills.

2. Using energy-efficient appliances: Many appliances today are designed to be more energy efficient than their older counterparts. Energy Star certified appliances, for example, use less energy and water than traditional appliances.

3. Adjusting thermostats: Heating and cooling systems account for a significant portion of energy usage in homes and buildings. By adjusting thermostats by just a few degrees, we can save energy and reduce our environmental impact.

    In addition to these habits, there are several other ways to conserve energy, such as using public transportation, carpooling, or walking instead of driving alone. Renewable energy sources like solar and wind power can also help reduce our dependence on fossil fuels.

Conserving energy not only reduces our environmental impact, but it can also save us money on utility bills. Additionally, energy conservation can lead to increased energy security by reducing our dependence on nonrenewable resources.

[!tip] Leadership Tip Working on weatherizing homes, replacing or installing fire safety equipment, or helping your neighbors upgrade their appliances are all great ways to show Environmental Leadership.

I don't know about you, but my energy bills have hiked upwards of 30% in the last few years. All of these conserving energy habits are essential, because my salary has not increased by 30% in the last few years.

9.1.3 Eating locally and seasonally

Eating locally and seasonally is another important habit for achieving sustainable living. The food we eat has a significant impact on the environment, from the resources required to produce it to the transportation used to get it to our plates. Eating locally grown and seasonal foods can help reduce this impact in several ways.

When we eat locally grown foods, we support local farmers and reduce the carbon footprint associated with food transportation. By purchasing produce that is grown close to home, we reduce the energy needed to transport it from faraway places. Additionally, eating seasonal foods means we are not consuming foods that have been grown in greenhouses or transported long distances, which require more energy and resources.

Eating locally and seasonally also has other benefits beyond sustainability. Locally grown produce is often fresher and more flavorful, as it is harvested at its peak and doesn't need to be stored for long periods of time. It also supports the local economy and helps create a sense of community around food.

There are several ways to start eating locally and seasonally, including shopping at farmers markets or joining a community-supported agriculture (CSA) program. These programs allow consumers to purchase fresh, locally grown produce directly from farmers. Additionally, growing your own fruits and vegetables in a home garden is another way to eat locally and seasonally.

If you're trying to save money, keep in mind that both CSAs and container gardening can get expensive quickly. Seeds-to-soil is about the only cheap gardening method out there. If you don't eat enough to justify a CSA or a whole garden, just check out your local farmer's markets. They're pretty great.

[!attention] Accessibility Keep in mind that "eating locally" can be a challenge for people who live in food deserts. A food desert is a place that doesn't have easy access to groceries. These are often concentrated in low-income communities of color. Community gardens and farmers markets are essential in these places, but those communities often go without.

[!tip] Leadership Tip True justice-focused environmental efforts around food security need to address food deserts. If you live in or near a food desert, working on the issue is a great way to show Environmental Leadership!

9.1.4 Using active transportation

Using active transportation is another important habit for achieving sustainable living. The transportation sector is a significant contributor to greenhouse gas emissions and air pollution, making it critical that we reduce our dependence on fossil fuels. Active transportation, such as walking, biking, or taking public transportation instead of driving alone, can help achieve this goal in several ways.

Walking and biking are sustainable modes of transportation that do not require fuel and have no carbon emissions. They also promote physical activity, which has numerous health benefits. Additionally, using public transportation, such as buses or trains, can significantly reduce the number of cars on the road and, consequently, reduce traffic congestion and air pollution.

Using active transportation requires a change in habits, but it can be a convenient and affordable alternative to driving alone. Walking or biking short distances, for example, can be a quick and easy way to get exercise and reduce one's environmental impact. Additionally, public transportation is often more cost-effective than driving and can save money on gas, parking fees, and vehicle maintenance.

In addition to being a sustainable and cost-effective alternative to driving alone, active transportation can also increase social connections and promote community building. Walking, biking, and taking public transportation allow individuals to meet new people and engage with their surroundings in new ways.

[!attention] Accessibility Many people with physical disabilities cannot walk or bicycle easily. Two suggestions for disabled folks and neighbors: electric scooters or chairs can provide no-car transportation boosts. And a tricycle or bicycle with pedal assist can provide some light exercise if you're able to pedal. Either of these options can help you avoid cars and get a little bit of sun while you're out doing your day.

Additionally, many cities are made for cars, not for human transport. One of the new local libraries here in Dayton (Ohio) opened with a bit of controversy because they placed it next to a very busy road. People did not feel safe crossing that road. In response to these complaints and advocacy efforts, the city teamed up with the library to provide free shuttles across the road during peak library hours.

9.1.5 Supporting sustainable products

Supporting sustainable products is another important habit for achieving sustainable living. Many products today are designed to be more eco-friendly or made from sustainable materials, and choosing these products can significantly reduce our environmental impact.

However, keep in mind that not everything marketed as sustainable actually is better for the environment. There are a few concepts worth knowing about in sustainability that may influence your choices.

9.1.5.1 *Leakage and Environmental Substitutes*

The concept of leakage is one. It's a gross phrase, but it basically means that if a product is NOT sourced from one sensitive habitat, it might just be sourced from another. If we prevent all logging in the US and Canada, then businesses may get their wood from the South American rainforest.

Leakage is especially important when we think about things like carbon sequestration and carbon markets. The idea of a carbon market is that you are buying credits of good things in one place, to offset the damage that you're doing in another. In practice, however, issues like leakage can completely negate any good you were trying to do.

[!attention] Environmental Justice These pay-to-play systems (like carbon markets) run the risk of overburdening communities with pollution. It basically allows a company to keep polluting a low-income community of color because they've protected a forest on the other side of the country.

9.1.5.2 *The Quality of Recycling*

Keeping an eye on the types of recycled materials ("pre-" or "post-" consumer) can also be informative. When consumers think of recycled items, they automatically assume that it's post-consumer. E.g., their new bottle of soda was made from their old bottle of soda. But this is rarely the case.

There's also degradation of post-consumer materials. For example, you can't make wood fibers longer in the recycling plants. Large chunks of cardboard can only be recycled into smaller pieces. You can't make printer paper out of toilet paper or tissues. It's basically a race to the bottom when it comes to post-consumer recycling, and eventually, we will pay the price for those materials.

9.1.5.3 Certifications and Greenwashing

Choosing products with eco-friendly certifications, such as Energy Star for appliances and Forest Stewardship Council for wood products, ensures that these products meet strict sustainability standards. These certifications help consumers make informed choices about the products they purchase and support companies that prioritize sustainability.

Certifications are a good start, but those, too, can be problematic. Certification standards tend to meet the lowest common denominator instead of keeping rigid standards. And some certification schemes are organized by the companies that are being held to them. It's another case of the fox supervising the hen coop. So do your research. Throw that certification scheme into Google and keep your eyes peeled for what critical voices are saying.

9.2 BEING RESPONSIBLE WITH RESOURCES

Being responsible with resources is an important habit for achieving sustainable living. Responsibility with resources refers to the practice of using natural resources in a way that conserves them for future generations. This involves understanding the impact of resource consumption and taking steps to reduce that impact.

Conserving resources such as water and energy is important for several reasons. Water scarcity is becoming increasingly prevalent, and it's estimated that by 2025, half of the world's population will be living in water-stressed areas. Conserving water, therefore, is critical for ensuring that there is enough water available for everyone. Similarly, energy consumption is closely tied to greenhouse gas emissions and climate change. By conserving energy, we can reduce our carbon footprint and mitigate the effects of climate change.

Strategies for responsible resource consumption include:

1. **Reducing water usage:** This can involve taking shorter showers, fixing leaks, and using low-flow fixtures.

2. **Conserving energy:** This can involve turning off lights and electronics when not in use, using energy-efficient appliances, and adjusting thermostats.

3. **Reducing paper usage:** This can involve using digital documents instead of paper, printing double-sided, and recycling paper products.

4. **Choosing sustainable products:** This can involve purchasing products made from sustainable materials or that have eco-friendly certifications.

5. **Composting:** This can involve taking organic waste materials such as food scraps, yard waste, and paper products and breaking them down into nutrient-rich soil.

   By adopting these strategies for responsible resource consumption, we can reduce our environmental impact and contribute to a more sustainable future. Additionally, responsible resource consumption often has economic benefits, such as lower utility bills and reduced waste disposal costs.

Being responsible with resources is an essential habit for achieving sustainable living. These habits can significantly reduce our environmental impact and contribute to a more sustainable future

9.3 Incorporating Sustainable Habits into Everyday Life

Incorporating sustainable habits into everyday life is essential for achieving a more sustainable future. However, adopting new habits can be challenging, especially when we are used to certain routines. Here are some tips for incorporating sustainable habits into daily routines:

1. **Start small:** Begin by making one small change at a time. This could be something as simple as bringing a reusable water bottle or coffee cup instead of using disposable ones.

2. **Make it convenient:** Choose habits that are easy to incorporate into daily routines. For example, if you want to start biking to work, make sure you have a safe and convenient route to your workplace.

3. **Seek support:** Surround yourself with people who support sustainable habits. This could involve joining a community group or finding friends who share your sustainability values.

4. **Educate yourself:** Learn about the impact of your daily habits on the environment and identify areas where you can make changes. This will help you develop a deeper understanding of the importance of sustainable living.

5. **Celebrate progress:** Recognize and celebrate the progress you make toward your sustainable living goals. This will help motivate you to continue developing sustainable habits.

Overcoming challenges in adopting new habits can be difficult but is an essential part of sustainable habit development. Common challenges include lack of motivation, difficulty breaking old habits, and feeling overwhelmed by the amount of change required. We have to remember that sustainable habit development is a journey, not a destination. It takes time, effort, and patience to incorporate sustainable habits into daily routines.

Creating an individualized plan for sustainable habit development can help overcome these challenges. Start by identifying your sustainability goals and the habits necessary to achieve them. Then, break down the habits into smaller, achievable steps and create a timeline for incorporating them into your routine. Consider tracking your progress and adjusting your plan as needed. This is also great reflective material for a portfolio or resume.

9.4   SHARING AND SPREADING SUSTAINABLE HABITS

Sharing and spreading sustainable habits is an important part of achieving a more sustainable future. By sharing our knowledge and experiences with others, we can inspire them to adopt sustainable habits and create a larger impact. Here are some reasons why it's important to share sustainable habits with others:

1. **Creating a ripple effect:** When we share sustainable habits with others, we create a ripple effect that can encourage others to adopt similar habits. This can have a larger impact than just one person making sustainable choices.

2. **Building a community:** Sharing sustainable habits is a great way to connect with like-minded people and build a community around sustainability. This can create a sense of

belonging and motivation to continue making sustainable choices.

3. **Spreading awareness:** Many people may not be aware of the impact their daily choices have on the environment. Sharing sustainable habits can help raise awareness and encourage others to make more informed choices.

   When it comes to sharing sustainable habits with others, it's important to do so in an effective and non-pushy way. Some effective ways to share sustainable habits include:

1. **Leading by example:** One of the most effective ways to inspire others is to lead by example. By living a sustainable lifestyle and explaining your choices to others, you can show them that sustainable living is achievable and fulfilling.

2. **Starting a conversation:** Engaging in conversations about sustainability can help raise awareness and encourage others to think about their lifestyle choices. Asking questions and listening to others' perspectives can also help facilitate meaningful discussions.

3. **Compassionate sharing:** No one likes a pushy vegan. Sharing articles, books, or documentaries about sustainability can help educate others and provide inspiration for sustainable living. But use your brain and only share with consent - when folks are genuinely interested.

4. **Creating a community:** Building a community around sustainability can be a great way to share ideas, tips, and experiences. This can be done through social media groups, local events, or community programs.

5. **Problem-solving:** Structural issues, like systemic racism or classism, may keep your neighbors for taking on more sustainable habits. Help problem solve, and determine what it is they need and want from the city, the community, and their other support systems.

To promote sustainable habits without coming off as pushy, it's important to approach the topic from a place of positivity and encouragement. Focus on the positive impact that sustainable habits can have and share your own experiences in a non-judgmental way.

9.5 CHALLENGES AND SOLUTIONS

Fostering sustainable habits can be challenging, especially in a world where convenience and consumerism are dominant values. However, it's essential that we overcome these challenges in order to achieve a more sustainable future. Here are some common challenges in fostering sustainable habits:

9.5.1 Lack of motivation

Lack of motivation is one of the common challenges in fostering sustainable habits. It's easy to get excited about making more sustainable choices initially, but maintaining that motivation over time can be difficult, especially when we're trying to adopt new habits that require effort and time.

One of the reasons for the lack of motivation could be that we don't see immediate benefits or rewards from our sustainable choices. It can be challenging to stay motivated when we don't see the positive impact of our actions right away. Another reason could be that we're not fully committed to the idea of sustainability and don't see how our actions can contribute to a larger goal.

To overcome the lack of motivation, it can be helpful to set achievable goals and celebrate progress along the way. Break down your sustainability goals into smaller, more manageable steps, and track your progress toward achieving them. Celebrate every small success, as this can help boost your motivation and maintain momentum towards your larger sustainability goals. Another way to stay motivated is to create a sense of accountability by sharing your goals with others. Whether through social media or in-person discussions, letting others know about your goals can provide additional motivation to stay on track.

It's important to remember that developing sustainable habits is a journey, not a destination. It takes time and effort to adopt new habits and make them a part of our daily routine. Be patient with yourself, and don't get discouraged if you slip up along the way. Remembering why you started on this journey and the impact your sustainable habits can have on the environment and future generations can help you stay motivated and committed to your sustainability goals.

9.5.2 Time constraints

Time constraints can be a significant challenge in adopting and maintaining sustainable habits, as many of these habits require more time and effort than their unsustainable counterparts. For example, cooking at home using fresh ingredients takes longer than ordering fast food or eating pre-packaged meals. Similarly, using public transportation or walking/biking to work may take more time than driving a car.

To overcome this challenge, it's important to find ways to make sustainable habits as convenient and efficient as possible. One strategy is to plan ahead by meal prepping for the week or batch cooking on weekends. This can save time during the week and make it easier to stick to healthy, sustainable eating habits.

Another strategy is to multitask while being sustainable. For example, you can listen to an audiobook or podcast while walking or biking to work instead of simply listening to music. This can make it a more enjoyable and productive experience.

In addition, it's important to remember that sustainable living is not an all-or-nothing proposition. Even small changes can have a significant impact over time. For example, if you can't commit to using active transportation every day, try doing so once a week or for shorter distances. Every little bit counts, and it's better to make small changes than none at all.

[!tip] Life Pro Tip It's important to cut yourself some slack. Our world is unbelievably busy, and with wage stagnation in the last 30 years, we have less time - and discretionary income - to make the changes we want. Ultimately, you need to do what you need to do in order to survive.

9.5.3   Social pressure

Peer pressure and social norms can make it difficult to stick to sustainable habits, especially if those around us do not share our values.

To overcome these challenges and maintain sustainable habits over time, it's important to develop strategies that work for you. Here are some effective strategies for maintaining sustainable habits:

1. **Set achievable goals:** Setting small, achievable goals can help maintain motivation and lead to larger changes over time.

2. **Develop routines:** Creating routines around sustainable habits, such as meal planning and using a bike to commute, can help integrate sustainable choices into daily life.

3. **Find alternatives:** Finding alternatives that are convenient and enjoyable can help overcome time constraints and increase motivation. For example, finding a favorite plant-based recipe or discovering a new walking route can make sustainable habits more enjoyable.

4. **Seek support:** Seeking support from others who share your values can provide motivation and accountability. This could involve joining a sustainability group, participating in community events, or finding a sustainability buddy.

    In addition to developing personal strategies, seeking support from others is an important part of maintaining sustainable habits. Connect with others who share our values, and we can find inspiration, motivation, and accountability. Additionally, building a community around sustainability can provide a sense of belonging and connection that can further motivate us to maintain sustainable habits.

[!tip] Leadership Tip If sustainability is what gets you going, think about a little neighborhood togetherness campaign. Something like "#SustainableFairfield" has a nice ring to it, and you can sub in your neighborhood.

> Fostering sustainable habits can be challenging, but it's essential for achieving a more sustainable future. By setting achievable goals, developing routines, finding alternatives, and seeking support from others, we can overcome challenges and maintain sustainable habits over time.

9.6 CONCLUSION

In conclusion, fostering sustainable habits is essential for achieving environmental sustainability. By adopting small but impactful changes in our daily lives, we can significantly reduce our environmental impact and contribute to a more sustainable future.

We've discussed various sustainable habits that can be incorporated into everyday life, such as reducing water and energy usage, supporting sustainable products, using active transportation, and being responsible with resources. We've also explored strategies for sharing and promoting sustainable habits with others while overcoming challenges.

It's up to each of us to take action and adopt sustainable habits in our daily lives. We encourage readers to start small, set achievable goals, and seek support from others. Every sustainable choice we make, no matter how small, has the potential to create a larger impact and inspire others to do the same.

I urge readers to take action and make a commitment to adopt and promote sustainable habits in their own lives. By doing so, we can work towards creating a more sustainable and equitable future for all.

For further learning on sustainable habits, I recommend checking out resources such as books, documentaries, and online communities that promote sustainability. Sustainable living is a journey, and there is always more to learn and discover along the way.

9.7 Reflective Questions

1. What are some of the challenges you face when trying to adopt sustainable habits into your daily routine?

2. Which sustainable habits discussed in this chapter do you currently practice, and which ones would you like to adopt in the future?

3. How can you overcome social pressure to adopt unsustainable habits and make more sustainable choices instead?

4. What motivates you to prioritize sustainable habits in your daily life?

5. How can you create routines that include sustainable habits, even when you have a busy schedule?

6. What are some strategies you could use to encourage others to adopt sustainable habits without coming off as pushy or judgmental?

7. How can you track your progress toward achieving your sustainability goals and celebrate your successes along the way?

8. What impact do you think your individual choices and habits have on the environment and the larger community around you?

9. How can you build a supportive community of like-minded individuals to help you maintain sustainable habits over time?

10. What resources can you use to continue learning about sustainable habits and ways to incorporate them into your daily life?

9.8 Suggested Activities

1. Conduct a personal sustainability audit: Take some time to reflect on your daily habits and identify areas where you could make more sustainable choices. Create a list of 3-5 sustainable habits you would like to adopt, and create a plan for

incorporating those habits into your daily routine.

2.   Connect with others who share your values: Seek out community groups or online communities focused on sustainability. Joining a group of like-minded individuals can help provide motivation, support, and accountability as you work to maintain sustainable habits over time.

3.   Share what you've learned: Choose one sustainable habit that you've adopted or would like to adopt and share it with someone else. This could be a friend, family member, or co-worker. Discuss the benefits of the habit and how you've been able to incorporate it into your daily routine. By sharing your experiences, you may inspire others to make more sustainable choices as well.

10 Understanding Corporate Power

Corporate power has a significant impact on the environment, both globally and locally. It refers to the ability of corporations to influence political, economic, and social systems in ways that benefit their own interests, often at the expense of the environment and communities. The effects of corporate power on the environment are undeniable, including pollution, deforestation, and climate change.

In this chapter, I will explore the concept of corporate power and its impact on the environment. I will delve into the ways in which corporations exert their power and how they can be held accountable for their actions. I will also examine the role of consumers and activists in challenging corporate power and promoting sustainable practices.

By understanding corporate power and its impact on the environment, we can work towards creating a more equitable and sustainable future for all. My hope is that this chapter will serve as a starting point for readers to learn more about the issue and take action to promote sustainability in their own lives and communities.

10.1 The Role of Corporations in Environmental Destruction

The impact of corporations on environmental destruction is significant and far-reaching. From polluting waterways to deforestation and climate change, the actions of corporations have a profound impact on the environment. Corporations contribute to environmental harm in a variety of ways, including:

10.1.1 Overconsumption of resources

This consumption of resources has significant environmental impacts, including deforestation, soil erosion, and climate change. Many corporations rely on non-renewable resources, such as fossil fuels, which contribute to air and water pollution and greenhouse gas emissions.

In addition, overconsumption can result in the depletion of important resources needed by local communities for survival, such as clean water and fertile land for agriculture. This can lead to conflicts over resources, social and economic inequality, and even displacement of entire communities.

To address the issue of overconsumption, it is important to encourage sustainable consumption patterns and promote the use of renewable resources. This can involve promoting energy efficiency, reducing waste, and finding alternative sources of energy and materials. Governments can also play a role in regulating resource consumption through policies and regulations, such as incentives for sustainable practices and taxes on non-renewable resources.

10.1.2 Use of hazardous materials

These hazardous materials can have devastating consequences for both the environment and human health. They can contaminate air, water, and soil, leading to health problems such as respiratory illnesses, cancer, and birth defects. Workers who are exposed to hazardous materials on the job may also be at risk of injury or illness.

To address the use of hazardous materials, it is important to promote the use of safer alternatives and encourage responsible waste management practices. Governments can play a role in regulating the use and disposal of hazardous materials through policies and regulations, such as bans on certain chemicals or incentives for companies to adopt safer practices.

Corporations can also take action to reduce their reliance on hazardous materials by investing in research and development of safer alternatives, and adopting environmentally friendly production practices. Corporations have a social responsibility to use alternative materials and processes that minimize environmental harm.

[!tip] Leadership Tip Corporations are often reluctant to make a switch until the benefits outweigh the costs. Learning to play up the benefits or push up the costs are critical Environmental Leadership strategies. Playing up the benefits looks collaborative; pushing up the costs looks adversarial. Both strategies can work in different settings.

10.1.3 Emissions and waste

The emissions and waste produced by corporations can have a significant impact on the environment. Greenhouse gas emissions contribute to climate change, which can result in rising sea levels, increased frequency of extreme weather events, and loss of biodiversity. Waste production can lead to pollution of land, water, and air, negatively impacting the health of both humans and wildlife.

To address this issue, it is important to promote sustainable production processes and reduce waste generation. This can involve investing in renewable energy, improving energy efficiency, and adopting circular economy practices, such as reducing, reusing, and recycling materials. Governments can play a role in regulating emissions and waste through policies and regulations, such as carbon taxes or waste reduction targets.

Corporations need to take action to reduce their emissions and waste by conducting environmental impact assessments, setting sustainability goals, and monitoring and reporting on their progress. Integrating sustainability into their operations is no longer optional, so corporations should reduce their environmental impact and contribute to a more sustainable future.

10.1.4 Advocating For Stronger Regulations

In addition, as citizens and activists, we can advocate for stronger regulations and policies that promote sustainability and hold corporations accountable for their actions. This can involve engaging with policymakers, participating in public protests and campaigns, and raising awareness about the impact of corporate power on the environment and human health.

It is also important to recognize that promoting sustainability and holding corporations accountable is not solely the responsibility of individuals. Governments, civil society organizations, and corporations themselves all have a role to play in promoting sustainable practices and reducing the negative impact of corporate power on the environment.

[!tip] Leadership Tip Being collegial with corporate employees does not prevent you from calling out bad behavior. Nor should it. As citizens, we are the first line of defense against corporate bad-practices. Even if we have a beer or two with the Vice President of so-and-so. Showing resolve in the face of cooperation - and sticking to your guns - is the hallmark of a great Environmental Leader.

10.2 GREENWASHING HIDES CORPORATE GREED

Greenwashing is a tactic used by corporations to make their products or practices appear more environmentally friendly than they actually are. This can have serious consequences for environmental sustainability, as it can mislead consumers into believing they are making sustainable choices when they are not. Greenwashing can take many forms, but some common tactics include:

10.2.1 Use of misleading language

The use of misleading language by corporations can be a significant obstacle to promoting sustainable practices and reducing the negative impact of corporate power on the environment. Terms such as "natural" or "eco-friendly" can create the impression that a product or practice is environmentally friendly, even if this is not the case.

One way to address the use of misleading language is to promote transparency and accountability. Governments can play a role in regulating language used by corporations through policies and regulations that require accurate labeling and advertising. This can help ensure that consumers have access to accurate information about the environmental impact of products and practices.

Corporations themselves can also take action to promote transparency and accountability by providing clear and accurate information about their products and practices. This can involve conducting environmental impact assessments, setting sustainability goals, and reporting on progress towards these goals in a clear and accessible way.

Individuals can also make a difference by educating themselves about the impact of different products and practices and supporting companies that prioritize transparency and accountability. By choosing products that are labeled accurately and that have a minimal impact on the environment, we can help shift the market towards more sustainable practices and hold corporations accountable for their actions.

[!warning] Heads Up Greenwashing can be insidious. Whenever a corporation is making an environmental claim, look closely at any appeals to authority (like certifying bodies), reports that are long and dense, and other ways that they may be trying to obfuscate the truth.

10.2.2   Misleading visuals

The use of misleading visuals can be a significant challenge when it comes to promoting sustainability and reducing the negative impact of corporate power on the environment. Corporations may use images of nature or greenery, for example, to create a false impression that their products or practices are environmentally friendly.

One way to address the use of misleading visuals is to promote transparency and accountability. Governments can play a role in regulating visual representations used by corporations through policies and regulations that require accurate labeling and advertising. This can help ensure that consumers have access to accurate information about the environmental impact of products and practices.

[!warning] Advocacy Strategy There is special recourse if a corporation is publicly held. Corporations cannot (and should not) lie to their investors. So graphics must not be intentionally misleading. If you think a corporation has broken the rules, contact an environmental law firm and file a complaint with the Securities and Exchanges Commission (SEC) or the Consumer Protection Bureau (CPB).

10.2.3 False certifications

The use of false certifications by corporations can be a significant challenge when it comes to promoting sustainability and reducing the negative impact of corporate power on the environment. These false certifications can create a false impression that a product or practice is environmentally friendly, even if this is not the case.

One way to address the use of false certifications is to promote transparency and accountability. Governments can play a role in regulating certifications used by corporations through policies and regulations that require accurate labeling and advertising. This can help ensure that consumers have access to accurate information about the environmental impact of products and practices.

Third-party organizations themselves can also take action to promote transparency and accountability by providing clear and accurate information about their certification processes and the environmental impact of products and practices. Consumers and civil society organizations can also play a role in holding third-party organizations accountable for their certifications.

Many times, certification schemes will exist, but their leadership is little more than an industry advocacy group. A great example is the Sustainable Biomass Partnership (SBP), which is little more than bioenergy companies certifying themselves as sustainable. While the SBP is allowed to exist, we don't need to give it social authority. You may not be able to improve the SBP, but you can pressure your local government to refuse to accept its credentials.

10.2.4 Company Research

It's important to be able to identify and call out greenwashing in order to promote environmental sustainability. One strategy for doing so is to research companies and their products before making a purchase. Look for independent third-party certifications or information about the company's environmental practices. If this information is not available, reach out to the company and ask for more information about their environmental impact.

Being wary of exaggerated claims and buzzwords is an important strategy for individuals to ensure they are making informed choices about the environmental impact of products and practices. Terms like "green" or "sustainable" can be vague or misleading, and do not necessarily provide accurate information about a product or practice's true environmental impact.

Instead, it is important to look for specific information about a company's environmental impact and practices. This may involve researching a company's environmental policies and practices, including their use of energy and water, their waste management processes, and their efforts to reduce greenhouse gas emissions.

Individuals can also look for specific certifications or labels that indicate a product or practice has met certain environmental standards or is environmentally friendly. However, it is important to research these certifications and ensure they are legitimate and relevant to the product or practice in question.

By being proactive and seeking out accurate and specific information about a company's environmental impact, individuals can make informed choices about the products and practices they support. This can help encourage corporations to prioritize sustainability and reduce their negative impact on the environment.

[!tip] Leadership Tip It's important to hold companies accountable for their actions and to support organizations and activists working to promote environmental sustainability. By calling out greenwashing and promoting genuine sustainable practices, we can work towards a more equitable and sustainable future for all. Corporate campaigning isn't for everyone, but you should always be wary when working with for-profit entities.

10.3 THE IMPORTANCE OF CORPORATE RESPONSIBILITY

Corporate responsibility is a crucial element in achieving environmental sustainability. By adopting sustainable practices and policies, corporations can significantly reduce their environmental impact and contribute to a more equitable and sustainable future for all.

There are many ways in which corporations can adopt sustainable practices and policies. Some strategies include reducing waste and emissions, sourcing materials sustainably, using renewable energy sources, and investing in sustainable technologies. In addition, corporations can prioritize transparency and accountability by publicly reporting on their environmental impact and setting measurable goals for improvement.

The benefits of corporate responsibility extend beyond the environment. Companies that prioritize sustainability are often better positioned to attract and retain customers who value sustainability, and may also see cost savings through reduced resource consumption and increased efficiency. In addition, companies that prioritize sustainability may be more resilient in the face of environmental challenges such as climate change or natural disasters.

It's important for consumers and activists to hold corporations accountable for their actions and to support companies that prioritize sustainability. When we choose to support sustainable companies, we can help shift the market towards more sustainable practices and reduce the impact of corporate power on the environment.

Holding corporations accountable for their impact on the environment is crucial for promoting environmental sustainability. There are many strategies for holding corporations accountable, including:

10.3.1 Pressure through social and traditional media

The use of social and traditional media can be a powerful tool for activists and consumers to draw attention to corporate practices that are harmful to the environment. By leveraging both social media platforms and traditional media outlets, individuals and organizations can reach a wide audience and raise public awareness about the negative impact of corporate power on the environment.

Social media platforms like Twitter, Facebook, and Instagram can serve as a platform for individuals and organizations to share information about corporate practices they believe are harmful to the environment. By using hashtags and other tools to promote their message, activists and consumers can amplify their voices and reach a wider audience.

Traditional media outlets like newspapers, television news, and radio can also play an important role in drawing attention to environmental issues and putting pressure on corporations to change their behavior. By reporting on environmental issues and highlighting the negative impact of corporate power on the environment, journalists can help raise public awareness and promote accountability.

[!tip] Leadership Tip Remember who your target is when you are designing a campaign. If you want your message seen by corporate leaders whose headquarters are in Nashville, TN, you should be looking for Nashville specific resources. National media exposure is good, but if you're trying to reach the leadership and they only read The Economist, then that's where you need to be.

By using both social and traditional media, activists and consumers can help create a culture of sustainability that encourages corporations to prioritize environmental sustainability and reduce their negative impact on the environment. This can ultimately lead to more sustainable practices and a healthier planet for future generations.

10.3.2 Legal action

Legal action can be a powerful tool for holding corporations accountable for their environmental impact. In cases where corporations have caused significant harm to the environment, legal action may be necessary to seek damages or force companies to change their practices.

Lawsuits can be filed by individuals, communities, or organizations that have been negatively affected by corporate practices. These lawsuits can seek compensation for damages caused by environmental harm or force companies to change their practices in order to reduce their negative impact on the environment.

In addition to seeking damages or injunctions, legal action can also help raise public awareness about environmental issues and put pressure on corporations to prioritize sustainability. By highlighting the negative impact of corporate power on the environment, legal action can help promote transparency and accountability among corporations.

However, legal action can also be a complex and expensive process that requires significant resources and expertise. Individuals and organizations may need to work with legal professionals and environmental experts in order to build a strong case and achieve their desired outcomes.

Overall, while legal action can be an important tool for holding corporations accountable for their environmental impact, it is not always the best or most effective option. Other strategies, such as promoting transparency and accountability and raising public awareness through social and traditional media, can also play an important role in encouraging corporations to prioritize sustainability and reduce their negative impact on the environment.

[!tip] Leadership Tip Lawsuits aren't only for corporations. All of the government agencies, like the EPA and the Army Corps of Engineers, get sued regularly. It's how we change agency-wide practices. Suing the government is a great way to use the checks-and-balances system to get a more equitable solution to environmental problems.

10.3.3 Shareholder activism

Shareholder activism is a strategy in which shareholders of corporations use their voting power to influence corporate behavior and push for more sustainable practices. Shareholders who own a significant portion of a company's stock can leverage their voting power to bring attention to environmental issues and encourage corporations to prioritize sustainability.

Shareholder activism can take many forms. Shareholders may submit proposals for consideration at annual general meetings, vote on proposals put forward by other shareholders or the company leadership, or engage directly with company management to advocate for more sustainable practices.

By using their voting power to push for sustainable practices, shareholders can help create a culture of sustainability within corporations. This can lead to changes in corporate policies and practices that reduce the negative impact of corporate power on the environment.

In addition to promoting sustainability, shareholder activism can also have financial benefits for companies. By prioritizing sustainability, companies may be able to improve their bottom line through reductions in waste, energy usage, and other costs associated with unsustainable practices.

10.3.4   Governmental regulations

Government regulations also play an important role in regulating corporate behavior. Regulations can set standards for emissions and pollution, require transparency and reporting on environmental impact, and provide incentives for sustainable practices. However, government regulations are often subject to political and economic pressures, and may not always be effective in promoting sustainable practices.

Consumer activism is another key strategy for promoting corporate responsibility. By choosing to support sustainable companies and holding companies accountable for their actions, consumers can help shift the market towards more sustainable practices. This can include boycotting companies with poor environmental records, supporting sustainable alternatives, and advocating for stronger government regulations.

Ultimately, it is through a combination of government regulations, consumer activism, and legal action that we can hold corporations accountable for their impact on the environment and work towards a more equitable and sustainable future for all.

10.4 CHALLENGES AND SOLUTIONS

Promoting corporate responsibility is not without its challenges. Some common challenges in promoting corporate responsibility include:

10.4.1 Resistance from corporations

Resistance from corporations can be a significant challenge when it comes to promoting environmental sustainability. Many corporations prioritize profit over environmental sustainability, which can make them resistant to changing their practices. This can make it difficult to hold corporations accountable for their negative impact on the environment and promote more sustainable practices.

One of the key reasons why corporations may be resistant to changing their practices is the belief that environmental sustainability will negatively impact their bottom line. Many corporations view sustainability as an added cost, rather than an opportunity to reduce costs and improve long-term profitability.

In addition, some corporations may be resistant to change due to the influence of stakeholders who prioritize short-term profits over long-term sustainability. Shareholders, executives, and other stakeholders may be more focused on maximizing immediate profits than on addressing the long-term impacts of corporate power on the environment.

Finally, resistance from corporations can also be driven by a lack of awareness or understanding of environmental issues. Without a clear understanding of the negative impact of corporate power on the environment, corporations may be less likely to take action to reduce their environmental impact.

[!warning] Heads Up Companies can get really aggressive and resort to "black hat" tactics when it comes to intimidating or silencing environmentalists. Make sure that you keep your personal information private, and understand what happens if you or your organization gets sued by a company. So called "SLAPP" suits (strategic lawsuit against public participation) serve as a tool of harassment and intimidation.

10.4.2 Political and economic pressure

Political and economic pressure can pose a significant challenge to promoting environmental sustainability. Government regulations and economic pressures may work against environmental sustainability, making it difficult for corporations to adopt sustainable practices.

Government regulations can be both a help and a hindrance to promoting environmental sustainability. While some governments have implemented policies and regulations aimed at reducing the negative impact of corporate power on the environment, these policies are not always effective or enforced. In addition, some governments may be resistant to implementing environmental regulations due to concerns about the impact on economic growth.

Economic pressures can also pose a challenge to promoting environmental sustainability. Many corporations operate in competitive markets where profit margins are thin, which can make it difficult to prioritize sustainability over short-term financial gains. In addition, corporations may face economic pressures from stakeholders who prioritize immediate profits over long-term sustainability.

Finally, global economic and political systems can also pose challenges to promoting environmental sustainability. Economic globalization has created a highly interconnected world where environmental impacts can cross borders and affect people thousands of miles away. This can create challenges for environmentalists, as different countries and cultures may have different priorities and approaches to environmental issues.

10.4.3 Consumer awareness

Limited consumer awareness is another challenge when it comes to promoting environmental sustainability. Many consumers may not be aware of the impact of corporate behavior on the environment or may prioritize other factors over environmental sustainability when making purchasing decisions.

One reason for limited consumer awareness is a lack of transparency from corporations about their environmental impact and practices. Without access to accurate and specific information, consumers may not be able to make informed decisions about which products and companies are more environmentally responsible.

In addition, many consumers may prioritize other factors over environmental sustainability when making purchasing decisions. For example, consumers may prioritize convenience, price, or brand loyalty over environmental concerns. This can make it difficult for companies that prioritize sustainability to compete in the marketplace.

Finally, limited consumer awareness can also be driven by a lack of education and awareness about environmental issues. Many consumers may not have access to reliable information about environmental issues, or may not understand the impact of their own actions on the environment.

Despite these challenges, it is important to continue raising awareness about environmental issues and promoting more sustainable consumer behavior. By educating consumers about the negative impact of corporate power on the environment and encouraging them to prioritize sustainability when making purchasing decisions, we can encourage corporations to adopt more sustainable practices and contribute to a more sustainable future for all.

To overcome these challenges, it is important to use a variety of strategies, including:

10.4.4 Advocacy and activism

Advocacy and activism are important tools for promoting environmental sustainability. Activists and consumers can put pressure on corporations through advocacy and activism, influencing public opinion and creating demand for sustainable products and practices.

One of the key ways in which activists and consumers can advocate for sustainability is by raising awareness about environmental issues and corporate behavior. This can involve sharing information about the negative impact of corporate power on the environment, as well as highlighting examples of more sustainable practices and products.

Activists and consumers can also put pressure on corporations through direct action, such as protests, boycotts, and social media campaigns. These actions can draw attention to the negative impact of corporate power on the environment and create public pressure for corporations to adopt more sustainable practices.

In addition, advocates and activists can work to influence public policy and regulations, pushing for stronger environmental protections and regulations that hold corporations accountable for their actions. This can involve engaging with policymakers and advocating for policies that prioritize sustainability and reduce the negative impact of corporate power on the environment.

Overall, advocacy and activism are powerful tools for promoting environmental sustainability and holding corporations accountable for their actions. By working together to raise awareness, create demand for sustainable products and practices, and push for stronger policies and regulations, we can contribute to a more sustainable future for all.

10.4.5 Collaboration and partnership

Collaboration and partnership are essential for promoting environmental sustainability. Cooperation and dialogue between corporations, government agencies, NGOs, and other stakeholders can be an effective way to promote sustainable practices and overcome political and economic barriers.

One key benefit of collaboration is the sharing of knowledge and expertise. Corporations, government agencies, and NGOs all have unique perspectives on environmental issues, and by working together, they can share ideas and best practices, leading to more effective and innovative solutions.

Collaboration can also help to overcome political and economic barriers to sustainability. By bringing together diverse groups with different perspectives and interests, collaboration can build consensus around sustainable goals and work towards solutions that benefit everyone.

10.4.6 Financial incentives

Financial incentives can be an effective way to encourage corporations to adopt more sustainable practices. Providing financial incentives for sustainable practices, such as tax breaks or subsidies, can help reduce the cost of adopting sustainable practices and make them more economically viable.

One key benefit of financial incentives is that they can help overcome economic barriers to sustainability. Many corporations operate in highly competitive markets where profit margins are thin, making it difficult to prioritize sustainability over short-term financial gains. By providing financial incentives for sustainable practices, governments and other stakeholders can help offset some of the costs of sustainability and make it more financially viable for corporations to adopt sustainable practices.

Financial incentives can also help to level the playing field for sustainable businesses. By providing financial support for sustainable practices, governments and other stakeholders can help smaller, sustainable businesses compete with larger corporations who may have more resources and economies of scale.

In addition, financial incentives can create a self-reinforcing cycle of sustainability. As more corporations adopt sustainable practices, the demand for sustainable products and services increases, creating new opportunities for sustainable businesses and driving further innovation in sustainable practices.

Finally, financial incentives can also help to create positive public relations for corporations that adopt sustainable practices. By highlighting their commitment to sustainability, corporations can improve their brand image and reputation, which can ultimately lead to increased sales and customer loyalty.

10.5 CONCLUSION

In conclusion, understanding corporate power is crucial for achieving environmental sustainability. Corporations have a significant impact on the environment and communities, and it is important to hold them accountable for their actions and promote sustainable practices.

Through this chapter, we have explored the ways in which corporations contribute to environmental destruction, the importance of corporate responsibility, and the strategies for promoting accountability and sustainability. We have also discussed the challenges and potential solutions to promoting corporate responsibility.

As individuals, we can play an important role in promoting corporate responsibility by supporting sustainable companies, advocating for stronger regulations, and holding corporations accountable for their actions. By working together with other stakeholders, we can create a more equitable and sustainable future for all.

I encourage readers to continue learning about corporate power and environmental sustainability. Take action in your personal and professional lives to promote sustainability and hold corporations accountable. Together, we can build a more sustainable world for ourselves and future generations.

10.6 Reflective Questions

1. How has this chapter changed your understanding of the impact of corporations on the environment?

2. What role do you believe corporations should play in promoting environmental sustainability?

3. How can consumers and activists hold corporations accountable for their environmental impact?

4. Do you believe that government regulations are effective in regulating corporate behavior? Why or why not?

5. What are some examples of companies that have successfully adopted sustainable practices?

6. How can collaboration between stakeholders be used to promote corporate responsibility?

7. What challenges do you think are most significant in promoting corporate responsibility, and how can they be addressed?

8. What strategies do you use to identify and avoid greenwashing when making purchasing decisions?

9. How can individuals, communities, and governments work together to promote sustainability and hold corporations accountable?

10. What actions will you take to promote corporate responsibility and environmental sustainability in your personal and professional life?

10.7 SUGGESTED ACTIVITIES

1. **Take Action:** Reflect on the strategies discussed in this chapter for promoting corporate responsibility, and think about how you can take action in your personal and professional life. You can choose to support sustainable companies when making purchasing decisions, advocate for stronger regulations, or hold corporations accountable for their actions through activism and advocacy.

2. **Sustainable Business Challenge:** Challenge yourself to identify and support sustainable businesses in your community. This could involve researching companies and products before making purchasing decisions, seeking out sustainable alternatives, or encouraging others to do the same.

3. **Collaborative Effort:** Work with others in your community to promote sustainability and hold corporations accountable. This could involve organizing a community event or campaign, networking with local organizations and activists, or partnering with local businesses to promote sustainable practices and policies. Remember that it is through collaboration and collective action that we can create meaningful change and promote a more equitable and sustainable future for all.

11 LEADING ENVIRONMENTAL CHANGE

Environmental change is the process of promoting practices and policies that reduce the negative impact of human activities on the environment and promote sustainability. It is a critical component of achieving environmental sustainability, which is the balance between meeting the needs of the present while ensuring that future generations can also meet their needs.

As environmental challenges become increasingly urgent, the need for effective environmental leadership has never been greater. This chapter will explore the concrete project-planning process, and it will apply to something as small as a project and as large as a campaign or organization.

We will also discuss the importance of self-reflection and personal growth in environmental leadership, as well as the challenges and barriers that must be overcome to achieve sustainability. At its core, environmental leadership is the act of working towards creating a more sustainable future for all.

11.1 STRATEGIES AND TACTICS FOR LEADING ENVIRONMENTAL CHANGE

To lead environmental change, individuals can act in different spheres, including personal, social, institutional, and political. In each sphere, there are specific strategies and tactics that can be used to promote sustainability and achieve environmental goals.

In the **personal sphere**, individuals can lead environmental change by making changes to their own lifestyle and behavior. This can include reducing energy consumption, minimizing waste, eating a plant-based diet, and using sustainable transportation. By modeling sustainable behavior, individuals can inspire others to make similar changes and create a culture of sustainability.

In the **social sphere**, environmental change can be led through building strong relationships with stakeholders and working collaboratively towards sustainability goals. This can involve working with businesses, community organizations, and other groups to develop sustainable solutions, share knowledge and resources, and advocate for policy changes.

In the **institutional sphere**, environmental change can be led by working within organizations and institutions to promote sustainability. This can involve developing sustainability policies and practices, promoting sustainable procurement, and building a culture of sustainability within organizations.

In the **political sphere**, environmental change can be led through advocacy and activism, working to influence public policy and regulations. This can involve engaging with lawmakers and policymakers, advocating for stronger environmental protections, and campaigning for sustainability initiatives.

It is important to tailor strategies and tactics to specific contexts, taking into account cultural, social, economic, and political factors. What works in one sphere or context may not work in another, and it is important to adapt strategies and tactics to best suit the needs and challenges of each particular situation.

To lead environmental change, individuals can use a variety of strategies and tactics across different spheres. Here are some examples:

11.1.1 Personal Sphere

- Reduce energy consumption by turning off lights and electronics when not in use, using energy-efficient appliances and light bulbs, and adjusting thermostats.
- Minimize waste by recycling, composting, and reducing single-use items like plastic bags, straws, and packaging.
- Eat a plant-based diet or reduce meat consumption to lower the carbon footprint of food choices.
- Use sustainable transportation options like walking, biking, carpooling, or taking public transit.

11.1.2 Social Sphere

- Build relationships with stakeholders like businesses, community organizations, and advocacy groups to work collaboratively towards sustainability goals.
- Share knowledge and resources with others to promote sustainable practices and solutions.
- Advocate for sustainability initiatives like renewable energy, green infrastructure, and waste reduction programs.
- Encourage others to adopt sustainable behaviors and practices through education and outreach.

11.1.3 Institutional Sphere

- Develop sustainability policies and practices within organizations to promote sustainable behavior and decision-making.
- Promote sustainable procurement by selecting environmentally-friendly products and services.
- Implement sustainable transportation options for employees such as bike racks and parking spaces for electric vehicles.
- Create a culture of sustainability within organizations through education, engagement, and recognition of sustainable practices.

11.1.4 Political Sphere

- Engage with lawmakers and policymakers to advocate for stronger environmental protections and regulations.
- Participate in public comment periods for proposed policy changes related to environmental issues.
- Lobby for sustainability initiatives at the local, state, and federal level.
- Participate in protests, marches, and other forms of activism to raise awareness and demand action on environmental issues.

  Understanding these contexts is critical for knowing what type of change you can effect and at what level. If you can only operate at the personal sphere, but want to enact political change, recognition is key. If you know where you want to go, you can chart a path to getting there.

11.2 Designing and Implementing Effective Campaigns, Projects, and Policies

Designing and implementing effective campaigns, projects, and policies is a critical aspect of leading environmental change. There are tons of resources out there on project planning, and to be honest, they can all apply in Environmental Leadership as well.

The important thing in developing and implementing plans is really to stay the course. Make sure that your planning toolbox (e.g., like the one below) is flexible enough to handle the bumps that life will bring you. Environmental campaigns are wildly unpredictable, and can be strongly influenced by local or national news and happenings.

If you have a project planning process you prefer, stick to that one. If you're looking for a change, check out the project planning process suggested below. It can apply to personal and political projects alike, and can work with a team of one or a team of twenty. Here are the steps involved in this process:

11.2.1 Step 1: Define the problem and set goals

Step 1 of designing and implementing effective campaigns, projects, and policies is to clearly define the environmental issue that needs to be addressed and set specific goals for addressing it. This step is critical for several reasons, including:

Clarity: Defining the problem and setting clear goals provides clarity and focus to environmental change efforts. It ensures that all stakeholders are working towards a common objective and helps to avoid confusion or misunderstandings.

Motivation: Clear goals can also be a source of motivation for individuals and organizations involved in environmental change efforts. When goals are achievable and well-defined, they can inspire people to take action and feel a sense of progress along the way.

Accountability: By setting specific goals, it is easier to hold individuals and organizations accountable for their role in achieving them. This can help to ensure that progress is being made and that resources are being used effectively.

Specificity: When defining the problem and setting goals, it is important to be as specific and measurable as possible. For example, instead of setting a goal to "reduce plastic waste," a more specific and measurable goal could be to "reduce the use of single-use plastic bags by 50% by the end of the year."

Additionally, it is important to consider the larger context when defining the problem and setting goals. This includes understanding the root causes of the issue, as well as any related social, economic, or political factors that may impact the ability to achieve the goals.

11.2.2   Step 2: Identify stakeholders

Step 2 of designing and implementing effective campaigns, projects, and policies is to identify the stakeholders who will be affected by the initiative and engage with them throughout the design and implementation process. Stakeholders are individuals or groups who have an interest in or impact on the issue at hand. This may include community members, businesses, policymakers, scientists, and environmental advocacy groups, among others.

Engaging with stakeholders is critical for several reasons, including:

Inclusivity: Engaging with stakeholders ensures that diverse perspectives and experiences are represented in the initiative's design and implementation. This leads to more inclusive and equitable outcomes that reflect the needs and interests of all stakeholders.

Collaboration: Engaging with stakeholders fosters collaboration and builds trust between different groups. This can lead to more effective communication, problem-solving, and decision-making throughout the initiative's life cycle.

Accountability: Engaging with stakeholders promotes accountability and transparency, as it ensures that all groups are aware of the initiative's goals, progress, and potential impacts.

Context: When identifying stakeholders, it is important to consider both the primary and secondary stakeholders. Primary stakeholders are those who are directly impacted by the initiative, while secondary stakeholders are those who may be indirectly impacted or have an interest in the initiative's success.

Once stakeholders have been identified, it is important to engage with them throughout the initiative's design and implementation process. This may include conducting stakeholder interviews, surveys, or focus groups to gather input and feedback, hosting community meetings or forums to discuss the initiative, or creating advisory committees that represent diverse stakeholder groups.

11.2.3 Step 3: Develop a plan

Step 3 of designing and implementing effective campaigns, projects, and policies is to develop a plan that outlines the strategies, tactics, and resources needed to achieve the goals. A well-developed plan is essential for ensuring that efforts are focused, coordinated, and efficient. When developing a plan, it is important to consider the following:

Strategies: Strategies are high-level approaches to achieving the goals. They reflect the overall direction and theory of change for the initiative. For example, a strategy for reducing plastic waste could be to promote the use of reusable bags and containers.

Tactics: Tactics are specific actions or activities that support the implementation of the strategies. They are often more detailed and actionable than strategies. For example, tactics for promoting the use of reusable bags and containers could include distributing free reusable bags at community events or partnering with local stores to offer discounts on reusable containers.

Resources: Resources include the people, funding, equipment, and other materials needed to implement the plan successfully. It is important to assess the availability of resources and develop plans to acquire or allocate additional resources as needed.

Timeline: Developing a timeline helps to ensure that progress towards the goals is being tracked and that milestones are being met. It also serves as a guide for allocating resources and coordinating efforts across different stakeholders.

Once the plan has been developed, it is important to communicate it effectively to all stakeholders involved in the initiative. This includes sharing the goals, strategies, tactics, resources, and timeline, as well as any potential risks or challenges that may arise.

11.2.4   Step 4: Implement the plan

Step 4 of designing and implementing effective campaigns, projects, and policies is to implement the plan by executing the strategies and tactics outlined in the plan. This step involves putting the plan into action and carrying out the tasks required to achieve the goals. When implementing the plan, it is important to consider the following:

Coordination: Implementing a plan requires effective coordination between different stakeholders involved in the initiative. This may involve delegating tasks, communicating progress, and coordinating efforts across different groups.

Adaptability: Plans may need to be adapted or modified as new information becomes available or unexpected challenges arise. It is important to remain flexible and adaptable to changes in the environment and adjust plans as needed.

Monitoring and Evaluation: Monitoring and evaluating progress towards the goals is critical for ensuring that efforts are on track and that adjustments can be made as needed. Establishing metrics for success and tracking progress towards them is essential for effective monitoring and evaluation.

During implementation, it is also important to maintain effective communication with stakeholders, providing updates on progress, milestones, and any changes to the plan. Regular communication helps to build trust and accountability between different groups involved in the initiative.

11.2.5 Step 5: Monitor and evaluate

Step 5 of designing and implementing effective campaigns, projects, and policies is to monitor progress towards the goals and evaluate the effectiveness of the strategies and tactics used. This step involves tracking progress towards the established metrics for success, assessing the effectiveness of the initiative's strategies and tactics, and making any necessary adjustments. When monitoring and evaluating an initiative, it is important to consider the following:

Metrics: Establishing clear metrics for success is critical for effective monitoring and evaluation. Metrics should be specific, measurable, achievable, relevant, and time-bound (SMART).

Data Collection: Collecting accurate and reliable data is essential for effective monitoring and evaluation. This may involve using surveys, interviews, focus groups, or other methods to gather feedback from stakeholders.

Analysis: Analyzing data collected during monitoring and evaluation helps to identify patterns, trends, and insights that can inform decision-making and guide future efforts.

Adjustment: Using the insights gained through monitoring and evaluation, adjusting the initiative's strategies and tactics as needed is essential for ensuring that the effort remains effective and impactful.

Overall, monitoring progress towards the goals and evaluating the effectiveness of the strategies and tactics used is a critical step in leading effective environmental change initiatives. By doing so, individuals and organizations can ensure that their efforts remain focused, adaptable, and impactful, leading to greater progress towards a more sustainable future.

11.2.6   Step 6: Adapt and revise

Step 6 of designing and implementing effective campaigns, projects, and policies is to use the evaluation results to adapt and revise the plan as needed to improve its effectiveness. This step involves using the insights gained through monitoring and evaluation to adjust the initiative's strategies and tactics, and ensure that it remains aligned with its goals. When adapting and revising a plan, it is important to consider the following:

Results: Using the results of the evaluation to identify strengths and weaknesses in the initiative's strategies and tactics can help guide revisions. Understanding what has been working well and where improvements are needed is key to an effective adaptation.

Flexibility: Being flexible and adaptable to changes in the environment or new information is essential when making revisions. Plans may need to be adjusted as new challenges or opportunities arise.

Stakeholder engagement: Engaging stakeholders in the adaptation process helps ensure that their perspectives and input are considered. This helps to create more inclusive and equitable solutions.

Communication: Clear communication about why and how the plan is being adapted is essential for maintaining accountability and transparency, and keeping stakeholders informed about progress.

Making adjustments based on monitoring and evaluation results can help ensure that the initiative remains focused and effective towards achieving its goals. It also helps to build trust among stakeholders and maintains momentum towards achieving the desired outcomes.

11.3 OVERCOMING RESISTANCE, APATHY, OR OPPOSITION

Leading environmental change can be met with resistance, apathy, or opposition from various stakeholders. Common challenges faced in leading environmental change include:

Resistance: Individuals or groups may resist environmental change due to perceived costs or inconvenience, lack of awareness or understanding, or skepticism about the effectiveness of proposed solutions.

Apathy: Some individuals may not be engaged in environmental issues due to lack of interest or awareness, or a feeling of helplessness in the face of complex environmental problems.

Opposition: Some stakeholders, such as businesses or political entities, may actively oppose environmental change due to perceived threats to their interests or values.

To overcome these challenges and lead effective environmental change, individuals can use several strategies, such as:

Effective communication: Use clear, concise, and persuasive messages to engage and inform stakeholders about the importance, benefits, and feasibility of environmental change.

Coalition building: Build alliances with like-minded individuals or groups to increase the impact and credibility of environmental change initiatives.

Targeted advocacy: Focus efforts on key decision-makers who have the power to enact change, such as lawmakers or executives of influential companies.

It is also important to recognize that overcoming resistance, apathy, or opposition is often a long and challenging process. Persistence and adaptability are essential qualities for environmental leaders. They must be willing to persist through setbacks and failures, and to adapt their approach as needed based on feedback and evaluation results.

Overall, while leading environmental change can be met with challenges, there are strategies and qualities that individuals can employ to overcome them. By persisting in the face of resistance, apathy, or opposition and adapting their approach as necessary, environmental leaders can create meaningful and lasting change for a more sustainable future.

11.4 CASE STUDIES IN ENVIRONMENTAL CHANGE LEADERSHIP

Case studies of successful environmental change initiatives can provide valuable insights into effective leadership strategies and tactics. Here are a few examples:

Case Study 1: The Montreal Protocol In the 1970s, scientists discovered that chemicals called chlorofluorocarbons (CFCs) were causing depletion of the ozone layer, which protects the Earth from harmful ultraviolet radiation. In response, governments and organizations around the world worked to reduce CFC production and use. This global effort culminated in the Montreal Protocol, an international treaty signed by 196 countries to phase out CFCs. The Montreal Protocol is widely considered one of the most successful environmental agreements in history, with CFC production and use reduced by 98%.

Case Study 2: The California Clean Energy Act In 2018, California passed legislation calling for the state to obtain 100% of its electricity from renewable sources by 2045, making it the largest economy in the world to commit to this goal. The California Clean Energy Act was the result of years of advocacy and coalition-building by environmental groups, policymakers, and businesses. The law has the potential to reduce greenhouse gas emissions and promote the growth of the renewable energy industry.

Case Study 3: The Plastic Bag Ban in Rwanda In 2008, Rwanda became one of the first countries in the world to ban plastic bags. The ban was met with resistance from some businesses and consumers, but the government persisted, imposing fines and promoting alternative packaging options. Today, Rwanda is considered a leader in sustainable waste management, with the plastic bag ban credited with reducing plastic pollution and increasing public awareness of environmental issues.

Each of these case studies involved different strategies and tactics, including policy changes, coalition-building, and innovative solutions. However, they all share a commitment to persistence, stakeholder engagement, and evidence-based decision-making. By analyzing these case studies and drawing lessons from their successes and challenges, environmental leaders can inform and improve their own efforts to lead environmental change.

Overall, case studies of successful environmental change initiatives can help to inspire and guide future efforts, highlighting the importance of collaboration, innovation, persistence, and evidence-based decision-making.

11.5 CHALLENGES AND SOLUTIONS

While environmental change can be a rewarding experience, it can also be met with numerous challenges. Here are some common challenges and strategies to overcome them:

11.5.1 Challenge #1: Lack of resources

Environmental change initiatives often require significant resources, including time, money, and expertise. Limited resources can be a significant challenge to achieving the desired outcomes of an initiative. Here are some ways in which limited resources may hinder progress:

Lack of Expertise: Initiatives may require specific technical expertise or skills that are not available within the organization or community implementing the initiative. This can result in delays or errors in implementation, ultimately affecting the effectiveness of the initiative.

Insufficient Funding: Securing adequate funding is often a major challenge for environmental change initiatives. Funding may be required for developing the initiative, implementing it, monitoring its progress, and evaluating its impact. Lack of funding can result in delays in implementation, a reduction in the scope of the initiative, or even a complete failure to achieve the goals.

Time Constraints: Achieving the desired outcomes of an initiative often requires a long-term commitment. However, many organizations and communities face time constraints, including competing priorities or a lack of dedicated staff or volunteers. This can result in delays in implementation and progress towards the goals.

Lack of Infrastructure: Implementing environmental change initiatives often requires infrastructure such as buildings, equipment, and transportation. Lack of infrastructure can make it difficult to implement initiatives effectively, especially in low-income or underserved communities where resources are already limited.

11.5.1.1 Solution

Seek out partnerships and collaborations with like-minded organizations or individuals. Pooling resources can increase impact and efficiency. Additionally, look for creative solutions that utilize existing resources in new ways.

11.5.2 Challenge #2: Resistance and opposition:

Environmental change initiatives often face resistance and opposition from various stakeholders who have different values and priorities. Resistance and opposition can arise due to a variety of reasons, including:

Lack of Understanding: Some stakeholders may not fully understand the importance of the initiative or the need for change. This may lead to skepticism or doubts about the initiative's effectiveness.

Economic Interests: Environmental change initiatives may conflict with economic interests, such as those of industries that rely on natural resources or produce waste. These stakeholders may resist change that could impact their bottom line.

Political Interests: Environmental change initiatives may also face resistance from politicians who have different priorities or are influenced by special interests.

Cultural Differences: Cultural differences can also play a role in resistance and opposition. Stakeholders from different cultural backgrounds may have different values and priorities that conflict with the initiative.

11.5.2.1 *Solution*

Use effective communication strategies to engage stakeholders and address their concerns. Consider the importance of building strong relationships based on trust and respect. Also, consider coalition-building efforts to band together with others who share similar goals.

11.5.3 Challenge #3: Complexity of environmental issues

Environmental issues can be complex, multilayered, and difficult to understand. The complexity of these issues can make it challenging to identify effective solutions. Here are some ways in which the complexity of environmental issues can pose a challenge:

Interconnectedness: Environmental issues are often interconnected and can have ripple effects that extend beyond their immediate impacts. Addressing one issue may require addressing multiple related issues simultaneously.

Scientific Uncertainty: Environmental issues are often characterized by scientific uncertainty, making it difficult to identify cause-and-effect relationships or to predict the outcomes of different actions.

Social and Economic Factors: Environmental issues are often influenced by social and economic factors, such as poverty, inequality, or political instability. These factors can exacerbate environmental problems and make it difficult to implement effective solutions.

Global Nature: Many environmental issues are global in nature, meaning that they transcend national boundaries and require international cooperation to address effectively.

11.5.3.1 Solution

Use data and evidence-based decision-making to identify the most effective strategies and tactics. Work with experts, scientists, and researchers to gain a deeper understanding of the problem and potential solutions.

11.5.4 Challenge #4: Burnout and fatigue

Leading environmental change is a long-term and often challenging process that requires significant effort and energy. This can lead to burnout and fatigue, which can negatively impact the effectiveness of initiatives. Here are some ways in which burnout and fatigue can pose a challenge:

Lack of Motivation: Burnout and fatigue can lead to a lack of motivation, making it difficult to sustain the effort required to achieve the desired outcomes of an initiative.

Reduced Productivity: Burnout and fatigue can also reduce productivity, making it more difficult to meet deadlines and achieve goals.

Decreased Engagement: Burnout and fatigue can lead to decreased engagement, reducing support for the initiative and making it more difficult to build momentum towards achieving the desired outcomes.

Loss of Creativity: Burnout and fatigue can also lead to a loss of creativity, making it more difficult to develop innovative solutions to complex environmental problems.

11.5.4.1 Solution

Prioritize self-care to maintain resilience. Seek support from family, friends, colleagues, or mental health professionals as needed. Additionally, take breaks when necessary, and celebrate small successes along the way.

By addressing these challenges and maintaining momentum through ongoing collaboration, effective communication, and self-care, individuals can lead effective environmental change initiatives and create a more sustainable future.

11.6 GROWING IN YOUR LEADERSHIP

Leading environmental change requires a multifaceted approach and a combination of different strategies and tactics across various spheres. From personal changes to policy initiatives, there are many ways to make a positive impact on the environment.

By engaging with stakeholders, using evidence-based decision-making, and being persistent, you can overcome challenges and create meaningful change. It is also essential to prioritize self-care and resilience to maintain momentum and avoid burnout.

As readers, it is vital to take on leadership roles in promoting environmental change. Whether it is through personal actions or advocacy at the institutional or political level, everyone can play a role in creating a more sustainable future.

While you may not always live and breathe the frameworks suggested above, they are tools for you to help yourself and others understand how to fix environmental problems. As always, the most important thing is to get your hands dirty and decide if what you've learned is applicable to how you want to do things in life. Practice makes you a secure, effective changemaker at all levels of influence.

11.7 REFLECTION QUESTIONS

1. How has reading about the challenges and solutions discussed in this chapter impacted your understanding of environmental leadership?

2. What challenges have you personally faced when trying to lead environmental change, and how have you overcome them?

3. Which of the strategies and tactics discussed in this chapter do you feel most confident in implementing? Which ones do you find the most challenging?

4. What role do you believe stakeholder engagement plays in leading effective environmental change? Have you actively

engaged with stakeholders before, and if so, what was your experience like?

5. How do you prioritize self-care and resilience when working towards environmental change? Have you experienced burnout or fatigue in the past, and if so, how did you address it?

6. How do you incorporate evidence-based decision making into your environmental leadership efforts? Are there areas where you could improve in this regard?

7. What lessons can you draw from the case studies discussed in this chapter? Are there any that particularly resonate with you?

8. How does your personal sphere intersect with your social, institutional, and political spheres in regards to environmental change? Are there areas where you could create more alignment between these spheres?

9. What are some creative solutions you have seen others use to overcome resource limitations when leading environmental change? How could you apply these ideas in your own work?

10. What is one action you can commit to taking as a result of reading this chapter and reflecting on your own abilities as an environmental leader?

11.8 SUGGESTED ACTIVITIES

1. Identify an environmental issue that you are passionate about and develop a personal action plan for making a positive impact. Consider the strategies and tactics discussed in this chapter and tailor them to your personal context.

2. Research and engage with an organization or advocacy group focused on environmental change. Attend a meeting or event and connect with other individuals who share your passion for sustainability.

3.   Organize a community event focused on promoting sustainable practices. Consider inviting local businesses, community organizations, and policymakers to attend and learn more about the importance of environmental change.

12 Cultivating Environmental Leadership in Others

Cultivating environmental leadership in others is a critical component of building a more sustainable future. Environmental leadership can be defined as the ability to inspire and motivate others to take action towards achieving environmental goals. It is an essential quality for those seeking to make a positive impact on the environment, and it plays a vital role in driving change towards a more sustainable future.

In this chapter, we will explore the importance of environmental leadership in achieving sustainability and provide strategies for cultivating environmental leadership in others. We will discuss the qualities of effective environmental leaders, including communication, collaboration, and vision-setting. We will also provide practical tips for developing leadership skills and creating opportunities for others to become environmental leaders.

By the end of this chapter, readers will have a greater understanding of the importance of environmental leadership and the role it plays in driving change towards a more sustainable future. They will also have practical tools and strategies for cultivating environmental leadership in themselves and others, helping to build a more engaged and empowered community of environmental leaders.

12.1 MENTORING, COACHING, AND EMPOWERING ENVIRONMENTAL LEADERS

Mentoring, coaching, and empowering others are effective approaches to cultivate environmental leaders. These approaches help individuals develop essential leadership skills, gain knowledge about environmental issues, and take action to address them. Mentoring and coaching provide support, guidance, and feedback to individuals on their leadership journey, while empowerment empowers individuals to take ownership of their development and build self-confidence.

To be an effective mentor or coach, it is important to have a good understanding of the qualities and skills that make for successful environmental leadership. Key skills and qualities include:

12.1.1 Listening

Active listening is the first and most important skill you can have as an environmental leader. You must be able to listen to community members and their problems. You must be able to listen to your collaborators and teammates and reflect on what they're telling you. And, you must be able to listen to the signals from the broader world to determine if something requires a strategy change.

There are lots of great resources on listening, and, like with most skills, practice makes perfect. One good exercise is "reflective listening", where you tell someone what you thought you heard them say. This has been used and abused by leadership and manipulation books before, so let's be clear. The best way to use reflective listening is NOT to persuade someone. Don't jump right into rebutting them when you've said what they said. Instead, ask if what you said was correct. And if it wasn't - ask for clarification.

Listening is about understanding. Without understanding a person's motivations or experiences, we can't expect to help them improve their situation. Good, active listening skills apply whether you're in a boardroom negotiating or whether you're talking to your kid about climate change. Plus, feeling heard feels good.

12.1.2 Communication

Effective communication is essential for cultivating environmental leadership in others. The ability to communicate complex ideas and inspire action is critical for driving change towards a more sustainable future. Environmental leaders must be able to communicate their vision, goals, and strategies clearly and effectively to a variety of stakeholders, including policymakers, community members, and other environmental leaders.

One important aspect of effective communication is the ability to tailor messaging to different audiences. This involves understanding the needs, interests, and values of the people you are communicating with and adjusting your messaging accordingly. For example, messages that resonate with policymakers may be different from those that resonate with community members or business leaders.

Another important aspect of effective communication is storytelling. Stories have the power to inspire and engage people in ways that statistics and data alone cannot. Sharing success stories and examples of environmental leadership in action can help to inspire others and build momentum for environmental initiatives.

In addition to tailoring messaging and storytelling, effective communication also involves listening actively to feedback and engaging in dialogue with stakeholders. This means being open to diverse perspectives and actively seeking out opportunities to collaborate and learn from others.

12.1.3 Collaboration

Collation is a critical component of environmental leadership. Environmental challenges are complex and multifaceted, requiring the involvement of diverse stakeholders from different backgrounds and disciplines to achieve common goals. Effective collaboration involves building trust, developing relationships, and working towards a shared vision.

One important aspect of effective collaboration is the ability to recognize and value diverse perspectives. This means actively seeking out input and feedback from stakeholders and creating opportunities for underrepresented groups to participate in decision-making processes. By incorporating diverse perspectives, we can develop more comprehensive and informed approaches to solving environmental challenges.

Another important aspect of effective collaboration is the ability to communicate clearly and transparently. This includes establishing clear goals, expectations, and timelines, and providing regular updates on progress and outcomes. Effective communication helps to build trust and maintain momentum for collaborative efforts.

In addition to valuing diverse perspectives and clear communication, effective collaboration also involves creating a supportive environment for collaboration. This means fostering a culture of respect, empathy, and trust, and providing resources and support to facilitate collaboration. For example, providing funding for collaborative initiatives, offering training and professional development opportunities, and creating platforms for sharing information and best practices.

12.1.4 Vision-setting

Vision-setting is a critical component of environmental leadership. A clear and compelling vision can inspire and motivate others to take action towards a more sustainable future. Successful environmental leaders are able to set a clear vision, communicate it effectively, and work towards achieving it through collaboration and innovation.

Setting a clear vision involves identifying priorities, goals, and strategies that are aligned with environmental sustainability. This means understanding the complex and interconnected nature of environmental challenges and developing a comprehensive approach to addressing them. Environmental leaders must also be able to articulate this vision in a way that resonates with diverse stakeholders and inspires them to take action.

Communicating the vision effectively involves tailoring messaging to different audiences, incorporating storytelling and other effective communication strategies, and engaging in ongoing dialogue and feedback. By communicating the vision in a clear and compelling way, environmental leaders can build momentum and inspire others to take action.

Overall, vision-setting is a critical component of environmental leadership. Vision-setting is the difference between a manager and director, between a follower and a leader. You need to be able to set a strong vision so that you can execute the plan. Communicating the vision is key, too, because otherwise it may seem that you've haphazardly ended up at a place, instead of intentionally leading the way forward. Vision-setting, in a way, is showmanship, but it's showmanship for the greater good.

12.1.5 Empathy

Empathy is a critical component of environmental leadership. Environmental challenges impact people from all backgrounds and walks of life, and effective leaders must be able to understand and relate to the experiences of others. This means recognizing and valuing diverse perspectives and creating an inclusive environment where everyone can contribute to the collective vision.

One important aspect of empathy is active listening. This involves not only hearing what others are saying, but also seeking to understand their perspectives and experiences. By actively listening to diverse stakeholders, environmental leaders can gain new insights and develop more comprehensive and informed approaches to solving environmental challenges.

Another important aspect of empathy is cultural competence. This means understanding and valuing different cultural backgrounds and experiences, and recognizing the intersectionality of environmental challenges with other social justice issues. Environmental leaders must be able to engage with diverse communities in ways that are respectful, inclusive, and culturally appropriate.

In addition to active listening and cultural competence, effective empathy also involves building trust and fostering relationships with stakeholders. This means creating opportunities for dialogue and collaboration, providing transparency and accountability, and engaging in ongoing communication and feedback.

12.2 Supporting Budding Environmental Leaders

Creating a supportive environment is also critical for cultivating environmental leaders. Leaders need to feel supported, encouraged, and inspired to take risks, make mistakes, and learn from them. This requires creating an environment where individuals can thrive and grow, where they have access to resources and support, and where they are recognized and valued for their contributions. Here are some tips for creating a supportive environment:

12.2.1 Provide opportunities for feedback

Providing opportunities for feedback is a critical component of cultivating environmental leadership in others. Feedback helps individuals to develop new skills, build self-confidence, and stay motivated towards achieving their goals. It is important to provide both positive and constructive feedback, as both can be used to improve and grow.

Positive feedback can be a powerful tool for building self-confidence and motivating individuals to continue their efforts. It is important to acknowledge and recognize the accomplishments of environmental leaders, whether they are big or small. Sharing success stories and highlighting achievements can inspire others to get involved and contribute to environmental initiatives.

Constructive feedback is equally important, as it helps individuals identify areas for improvement and develop new skills. Constructive feedback should be specific, actionable, and delivered in a supportive manner. It is important to focus on behaviors and actions rather than personal characteristics, and to provide clear guidance on how to improve.

In addition to providing feedback, it is also important to create a culture of feedback in which individuals are comfortable giving and receiving feedback. This means creating an environment where individuals feel safe and supported in sharing their thoughts and ideas, and where feedback is seen as a learning opportunity rather than a criticism.

Overall, providing opportunities for feedback is an essential component of cultivating environmental leadership in others. Positive feedback can help to build self-confidence and motivation, while constructive feedback can help individuals to develop new skills and improve their performance.

[!tip] Leadership Tip The "sandwich" method of providing feedback is better than focusing only on negatives or areas of improvement. The sandwich method encourages you to provide positive feedback (and preferably a lot of it) first and last, with some constructive tips layered in between. If someone comes away from the experience feeling negative, it will impact their trust in you as their leader. Staying positive and encouraging and developmental with your teammates can help avoid trust issues altogether.

12.2.2 Encourage networking

Encouraging networking is a critical component of cultivating environmental leadership in others. Networking provides individuals with opportunities to build relationships, share ideas and best practices, gain inspiration and motivation, and learn new things. It is an important way to connect with other environmental leaders who share a similar vision and passion for sustainability.

One way to encourage networking is by creating opportunities for individuals to connect and collaborate. This can include attending conferences, joining professional organizations, participating in online forums and social media groups, and networking events. By providing opportunities for networking, individuals can expand their knowledge and connect with like-minded individuals who can provide support and guidance.

[!tip] Leadership Tip As the leader of an environmental group (department, business, organization, whatever) – you're in charge of making sure that your mentees get networking opportunities. Here, as in many aspects of business, money talks. Plan to set aside some money for travel to conferences, to pay for online networking spaces, or to create your own networking events for your mentees.

Another way to encourage networking is by fostering a culture of collaboration and knowledge sharing within the organization. This means creating opportunities for individuals to work together on environmental initiatives, sharing success stories and best practices, and providing opportunities for peer-to-peer learning. By fostering collaboration within the organization, individuals can build relationships and develop new skills that can benefit both themselves and the organization as a whole.

In addition to creating opportunities for networking and fostering collaboration within the organization, it is also important to encourage individuals to seek out mentorship and sponsorship opportunities. Mentorship and sponsorship can provide individuals with guidance, support, and connections that can help them to grow and develop as environmental leaders.

[!tip] Leadership Tip Resume review, LinkedIn mentorship, and other social networking tips are very important for people that you're mentoring. Bake these into the relationship that you have with your mentees, so that they feel comfortable talking about their careers beyond their involvement with you.

Overall, encouraging networking is an essential component of cultivating environmental leadership in others. By providing opportunities for networking, fostering a culture of collaboration, and encouraging mentorship and sponsorship, we can build a community of environmental leaders who are equipped to drive change towards a more sustainable future.

12.2.3 Provide access to resources

Providing access to resources is a critical component of cultivating environmental leadership in others. Access to resources such as funding, training, and information can help individuals build the skills and knowledge they need to become effective environmental leaders.

Funding is essential for many environmental initiatives, and providing access to funding opportunities can help individuals to develop and implement their own sustainability projects. This can include grants, loans, and other financial support that can help individuals get their ideas off the ground and make a positive impact on the environment.

Training is another important resource that can help individuals build the skills and knowledge they need to become effective environmental leaders. This can include training programs on topics such as sustainability, leadership, communication, and project management. Providing access to training opportunities can help individuals to develop new skills and confidence, and to apply these skills to real-world environmental challenges.

[!tip] Leadership Tip Access to information is also critical for environmental leaders. This includes access to data, research, and best practices that can help individuals to stay informed and up-to-date on the latest trends and developments in the field. Providing access to information can help individuals to make informed decisions, develop evidence-based solutions, and stay engaged with the broader environmental community. Set aside a budget, or set up a little "this is where you go to find what you need" session for any mentees you have.

Overall, providing access to resources is an essential component of cultivating environmental leadership in others. When we provide access to funding, training, and information, we empower individuals to take action towards a more sustainable future, and to become effective environmental leaders in their own right.

12.3 Creating and Sustaining a Culture of Environmental Leadership

Creating and sustaining a culture of environmental leadership is crucial for driving change towards a more sustainable future. Such a culture can help build momentum for environmental initiatives, create opportunities for collaboration and innovation, and promote the development of essential leadership skills. Whether in communities, organizations, or networks, creating and sustaining a culture of environmental leadership involves a variety of strategies and tactics.

12.3.1 Shared Sustainability Values

One approach to creating a culture of environmental leadership is to develop a shared vision and values regarding sustainability. This involves bringing together stakeholders to discuss and agree on a common set of goals and principles. It also involves communicating that vision and values widely, through messaging, storytelling, and other forms of engagement.

12.3.2 Cultural Leadership Development Resources

Another tactic is to create opportunities for leadership development, such as mentoring, coaching, and training programs. By providing individuals with the resources they need to develop leadership skills, organizations and communities can build a pipeline of environmental leaders who are equipped to drive change.

In addition to leadership development, creating a culture of environmental leadership involves recognizing and celebrating the contributions of environmental leaders. This can involve awards, recognition events, and other forms of acknowledgment. By highlighting the successes of environmental leaders, organizations and communities can inspire others to follow in their footsteps.

12.3.3 Progress Reports

To sustain a culture of environmental leadership, ongoing engagement and communication are critical. This includes providing regular updates on progress towards sustainability goals, sharing success stories, and creating opportunities for ongoing learning and growth. Regular engagement helps to keep environmental issues top of mind and reinforces the importance of leadership in driving change.

A culture of environmental leadership means making leaders out of everyone you meet. Anyone who participates in your group or organization should have a chance to be present for leadership opportunities. Every moment in the culture you're building is modeling and reinforcing that culture for others.

12.4 Leveraging Diversity, Equity, and Inclusion for Environmental Justice

Diversity, equity, and inclusion (DEI) are critical components of environmental leadership that promote environmental justice. DEI ensures that all individuals, regardless of their background, have an equal voice in decision-making processes and access to resources needed to address environmental challenges. The principles of DEI also help to generate a more comprehensive and informed approach to problem-solving.

One way to leverage DEI for environmental justice is to ensure that diverse perspectives are represented in decision-making processes. This involves creating opportunities for underrepresented groups to participate in environmental leadership roles and ensuring that their voices are heard and valued. It also involves taking into account the unique perspectives and experiences of diverse communities when designing and implementing environmental initiatives.

Another approach is to focus on equity and access to resources. This means ensuring that individuals and communities have access to the resources needed to address environmental challenges, such as funding, training, and information. It also means addressing systemic barriers that may prevent underrepresented groups from accessing these resources, such as racial and gender-based discrimination.

Many of the other leadership qualities and strategies discussed apply here as well. Active listening, collaboration with communities, and even understanding the political power system can all contribute to forming a more equitable culture.

Promoting DEI in environmental leadership can be challenging, especially given historical disparities in access to resources and decision-making power. Strategies for overcoming these challenges include:

12.4.1 Building Partnerships

Building partnerships with community-based organizations and leaders to ensure that all voices are represented in decision-making processes. We are all working together, and not in competition, with one another. That means it shouldn't matter if there are five other environmental organizations working on similar issues, because collaboration is more important than competition. This, of course, assumes shared values around Diversity, Equity and Inclusion. I'm not asking you to bring misogynists to the table because they use reusable napkins.

Partnering with community-based organizations can help to bring diverse perspectives and experiences to the table, and to ensure that decisions are made with input from those who are most impacted by environmental challenges. By building strong partnerships with community-based organizations, environmental leaders can work together to address environmental issues in ways that are equitable, inclusive, and sustainable.

12.4.2   Providing Resources

In addition to partnering with community-based organizations, environmental leaders should be aware of the power dynamics. Community-based organizations are often small or volunteer-run. If your organization has the resources, you need to step up and help them out.

It could be as informal as offering communications consulting, or as formal as becoming a grantor to support their work. Whichever path you choose, providing resources for smaller organizations will ultimately amplify the work that you're trying to do, too.

12.4.3   Prioritizing DEI

Providing resources and training to support underrepresented groups in leadership roles is a critical component of cultivating environmental leadership in others. This includes individuals from marginalized communities, including people of color, women, LGBTQ+ individuals, and low-income individuals, who may face unique barriers to accessing leadership opportunities.

Providing resources can include financial support, such as scholarships or grants, to help individuals overcome financial barriers to leadership development. It can also include access to training and mentorship programs that are designed specifically for underrepresented groups, providing them with the skills and knowledge they need to become effective environmental leaders.

Training programs can help individuals develop essential leadership skills, such as communication, project management, and strategic thinking. Mentorship programs can provide individuals with guidance, support, and connections that can help them navigate the complex landscape of environmental leadership and make a positive impact on the environment.

In addition to providing resources and training, it is important to create a culture of inclusion and equity within environmental organizations and initiatives. This means creating opportunities for underrepresented groups to participate in decision-making processes, providing space and support for diverse perspectives and experiences, and actively working to address the systemic barriers that limit access to leadership opportunities.

12.4.4 Ongoing Evaluation

Engaging in ongoing evaluation is a critical component of upholding DEI (Diversity, Equity, and Inclusion) principles in environmental leadership. Ongoing evaluation involves regularly assessing the effectiveness of DEI practices and policies, and making adjustments as needed to ensure that they are being upheld.

One way to engage in ongoing evaluation is by conducting regular assessments of organizational culture and climate. This can involve collecting feedback from employees, stakeholders, and community members to gain insights into how DEI principles are being upheld, and to identify areas for improvement.

In addition to assessing organizational culture and climate, it is important to evaluate the impact of DEI initiatives and policies on the broader community. This can involve tracking progress towards diversity and inclusion goals, monitoring the representation of underrepresented groups in leadership roles, and assessing the impact of environmental initiatives on diverse communities.

Engaging in ongoing evaluation also requires a commitment to transparency and accountability. This means sharing data and information with stakeholders, being open to feedback and critique, and taking action when necessary to address shortcomings or failures to uphold DEI principles.

12.5 Case Studies in Cultivating Environmental Leadership

There are numerous examples of successful environmental leadership initiatives that have cultivated leadership in others. These case studies provide valuable insights into the approaches used to cultivate environmental leadership and their impact on driving change towards a more sustainable future.

12.5.1 Green Ambassadors

One successful initiative is the Green Ambassadors program at Environmental Charter Schools (ECS) in Los Angeles, California. This program provides high school students with leadership training, project management skills, and mentorship from professionals in the environmental field. Through the program, students develop and implement environmental projects in their communities, building critical skills and gaining experience in environmental leadership. The program has been successful in cultivating a cohort of young environmental leaders who are making a difference in their communities.

12.6 CLIMATE REALITY LEADERSHIP CORP

Another example is the Climate Reality Leadership Corps, a global network of climate leaders who have been trained by former Vice President Al Gore to communicate about climate change and drive action in their communities. The program has been successful in building a community of environmental leaders who are equipped with the skills and knowledge needed to communicate about climate change effectively and drive action in their communities.

Lessons learned from these case studies include:

- Providing training and mentorship opportunities are effective ways to cultivate environmental leadership in individuals, especially youth.

- Focusing on leadership development across diverse sectors and settings can help to build a pipeline of environmental leaders who can drive change in different contexts.

- Building a community of environmental leaders can create a sense of shared responsibility and motivation for achieving environmental goals.

- Leveraging technology and innovation can be an effective way to engage and inspire individuals in environmental leadership roles.

     Overall, these case studies demonstrate the importance of cultivating environmental leadership in others and provide valuable insights into the approaches that can be used to do so effectively. By providing training, mentorship, and networking opportunities, we can build a community of environmental leaders who are equipped to drive change towards a more sustainable future.

12.7 Challenges and Solutions

Cultivating environmental leadership in others is a complex and challenging process that requires ongoing effort and adaptation. Common challenges in cultivating environmental leadership include:

- **Lack of resources:** Limited funding, staffing, and access to training opportunities can make it difficult for organizations and communities to provide the necessary support for developing environmental leaders.

- **Resistance to change:** Some individuals and organizations may be resistant to change or may not see the value in investing in environmental leadership development.

- **Lack of diversity, equity, and inclusion:** Barriers to entry and systemic biases can prevent underrepresented groups from accessing leadership roles and development opportunities.

     To overcome these challenges, organizations and communities can implement several strategies, including:

- Building partnerships with community-based organizations to share resources and collaborate on leadership development initiatives.

- Prioritizing diversity, equity, and inclusion in all aspects of environmental leadership development, including recruitment, training, and decision-making processes.

- Establishing clear goals and metrics for measuring success and evaluating the impact of leadership development initiatives.

- Providing ongoing training and professional development opportunities to support continuous learning and growth.

Ongoing learning and adaptation are also critical for maintaining momentum and achieving long-term success in cultivating environmental leadership. This includes regularly evaluating and adapting leadership development programs to ensure that they remain effective and relevant. It also involves creating opportunities for ongoing learning and growth, such as mentorship programs, networking events, and online resources.

Cultivating environmental leadership in others is a challenging but essential component of driving change towards a more sustainable future. Together, we can build a community of environmental leaders who are equipped to make a positive impact on the environment and drive change towards a more sustainable future.

12.8 Cultivating Leaders Is Solving Tomorrow's Problems

In conclusion, cultivating environmental leadership in others is an essential component of building a more sustainable future. Through mentoring, coaching, and empowering individuals, creating and sustaining a culture of environmental leadership, leveraging diversity, equity, and inclusion, and overcoming common challenges, we can build a community of environmental leaders who are equipped to drive change towards a more sustainable future.

You are encouraged to identify and take on leadership development roles in your own communities, organizations, or networks. By seeking out opportunities for leadership development, advocating for DEI in decision-making processes, and engaging in ongoing learning and growth, readers can make a positive impact on the environment and inspire others to do the same.

In summary, some key takeaways to consider are:

- Mentoring, coaching, and empowering individuals help to build essential leadership skills and drive change towards a more sustainable future.

- Creating a culture of environmental leadership involves developing a shared vision, providing leadership development opportunities, recognizing the contributions of environmental leaders, and engaging in ongoing communication and reflection.

- Leveraging diversity, equity, and inclusion can promote environmental justice and create more just and equitable outcomes for both the environment and communities impacted by environmental challenges.

- Overcoming challenges involves building partnerships, prioritizing DEI, establishing clear goals and metrics, and providing ongoing training and development opportunities.

  Finally, resources such as training programs, mentorship opportunities, and online resources can be valuable tools for those seeking to cultivate environmental leadership in themselves and others. When we work to build a community of environmental leaders, we create a more sustainable and just world for future generations.

12.9 REFLECTIVE QUESTIONS

1. What are some leadership skills that you would like to develop to become a more effective environmental leader?

2. How can you promote diversity, equity, and inclusion in your own leadership development initiatives?

3. What challenges do you anticipate encountering when cultivating environmental leadership in others, and how can you overcome them?

4. How can you leverage technology and innovation to engage and inspire others in environmental leadership roles?

5. What are some successful environmental leadership initiatives that you can learn from and apply to your own work?

6. How can you create a supportive environment for leadership development in your community or organization?

7. What steps can you take to ensure that diverse perspectives are represented in decision-making processes related to environmental issues?

8. How can you measure the impact of your leadership development initiatives and use that information to improve future efforts?

9. How can you continue to learn and grow as an environmental leader, even as you mentor, coach, and empower others?

10. What motivates you to cultivate environmental leadership in others, and how can you use that motivation to drive change towards a more sustainable future?

12.10 SUGGESTED ACTIVITIES

1. **Develop a leadership development plan** for yourself, including specific goals, training opportunities, and strategies for overcoming challenges.

2. **Organize a workshop or training program** to provide leadership development opportunities to individuals in your community or organization.

3. **Collaborate with other organizations or community groups** to create a shared vision and values around environmental sustainability, and develop a plan for achieving that vision.

13 ENVISIONING THE FUTURE OF ENVIRONMENTAL LEADERSHIP

Environmental leadership has evolved significantly over time, reflecting the changing social, economic, and political landscape of environmental issues. At its core, environmental leadership involves the ability to inspire and mobilize individuals and communities towards a more sustainable future. It requires an understanding of complex environmental challenges, as well as the skills and knowledge needed to develop effective solutions.

In this chapter, we will explore the future of environmental leadership and what it means for individuals, organizations, and society as a whole. We will examine current trends and emerging issues in environmental leadership, including the role of technology, the importance of diversity and equity, and the need for collaborative approaches to environmental problem-solving.

We will also explore how environmental leaders can adapt to meet these challenges and opportunities, by developing new skills and approaches to leadership, embracing innovation and creativity, and fostering a culture of inclusivity and collaboration. Finally, we will explore the potential impact of environmental leadership on the broader social and economic landscape, and reflect on the role that individuals and organizations can play in driving change towards a more sustainable and equitable future.

13.1 EMERGING TRENDS AND INNOVATIONS IN ENVIRONMENTAL LEADERSHIP

Emerging trends and innovations in environmental leadership are transforming the way we approach sustainability and environmental problem-solving. These new approaches are responding to the increasing complexity of environmental challenges, and the need for more holistic and integrated solutions.

13.1.1 Regenerative Design

Regenerative design is gaining momentum as an innovative approach to environmental leadership that can help to address the complex challenges of sustainability in a rapidly changing world. At its core, regenerative design seeks to restore and renew natural systems, rather than simply minimizing human impact on the environment.

This approach recognizes that human systems are interconnected with natural systems, and that restoring and improving natural systems can have positive impacts on social and economic well-being. Regenerative design emphasizes the importance of working with nature, rather than against it, and of creating systems that are resilient, adaptable, and sustainable over the long term.

Regenerative design can be applied across a wide range of contexts, from urban planning and architecture to agriculture and energy production. By prioritizing the restoration and renewal of natural systems, regenerative design can help to create more sustainable and equitable systems that benefit both people and the planet.

13.1.2 The Circular Economy

The circular economy has emerged as a powerful approach to environmental leadership that seeks to transform traditional linear systems of production and consumption into closed-loop systems that maximize resource efficiency and minimize waste.

At its core, the circular economy model is based on the concept of closed-loop systems, where waste is minimized, and materials are kept in use for as long as possible. This involves rethinking the design of products, processes, and systems to eliminate waste and optimize resource use.

The circular economy can be applied across a wide range of sectors, from manufacturing and retail to energy and transportation. By embracing this model, businesses and organizations can create more sustainable and resilient systems that benefit both the environment and the economy.

Key strategies for implementing the circular economy include designing products for durability and repairability, promoting reuse and refurbishment, and investing in recycling and waste reduction technologies. With the circular economy, businesses and organizations can reduce their environmental footprint while also creating new economic opportunities and driving innovation.

13.1.3 Social Entrepreneurship

Social entrepreneurship is an innovative approach to environmental leadership that combines business principles with social and environmental goals. Social entrepreneurs are committed to making a positive impact on society and the environment, while also generating economic value and creating sustainable jobs.

By leveraging the power of business to tackle social and environmental challenges, social entrepreneurs are driving change across a wide range of sectors, from energy and transportation to agriculture and finance.

Key strategies for social entrepreneurship include prioritizing sustainability and equity, embracing innovation and creativity, and investing in community building and partnerships. By prioritizing these strategies, social entrepreneurs can develop new approaches to problem-solving that are both effective and sustainable over the long term.

13.1.4 Citizen Science

Citizen science is an emerging trend in environmental leadership that involves the participation of everyday individuals in scientific research and data collection. By engaging citizens in the process of scientific discovery, citizen science can help to create a broader understanding of environmental issues and the creation of community-driven solutions.

Citizen science projects can take many different forms, including field research, data collection, and analysis, and the development of new tools and technologies. These projects can be designed to address a wide range of environmental challenges, from monitoring air and water quality to tracking species populations and migration patterns.

Key benefits of citizen science include increased engagement and education among the public, improved data collection and analysis, and the development of community-based solutions to complex environmental problems. Citizen science can also foster a sense of connection and stewardship among participants, helping to build stronger communities and a more sustainable future.

These emerging trends and innovations have the potential to make a significant impact on global sustainability. Regenerative design, circular economy principles, social entrepreneurship, and citizen science all have great value, but only if they continue to evolve.

We must stay informed and adaptable in the face of these emerging trends and innovations. Environmental leaders should remain open to new ideas and approaches, and be willing to learn and adapt as the field of environmental leadership evolves.

13.2 SHAPING THE FUTURE OF ENVIRONMENTAL LEADERSHIP

Individuals and communities play a crucial role in shaping the future of environmental leadership. As individuals, we have the power to drive change by advocating for policies and practices that promote sustainability and environmental justice. As members of communities, we can work together to create innovative solutions to complex environmental challenges and to build more resilient and sustainable systems. Finally, as leaders, we have the ability to drive change and guide the systems to a more sustainable and environmentally friendly place.

13.2.1 Advocacy

Advocacy is a crucial way for individuals and communities to participate in shaping the future of environmental leadership. By speaking out on issues related to the environment and advocating for policies and practices that promote sustainability and environmental justice, we can drive real change and create a more sustainable and just future.

One way to engage in advocacy is by contacting elected officials and policymakers to express your views on environmental issues and urge them to take action. This can involve writing letters, making phone calls, or attending public hearings and meetings.

Joining environmental organizations and campaigns is another effective way to engage in advocacy. By collaborating with like-minded individuals and groups, you can amplify your voice and work towards common goals related to sustainability and environmental justice.

Public education and outreach are also important components of advocacy. By raising awareness about environmental issues and educating others about the importance of sustainability and conservation, you can help to create a more informed and engaged community that is committed to driving positive change.

Advocacy has its roots in the Roman Empire and before, and it's certainly not going away anytime soon. Being convincing, communicating urgency, and being trustworthy are all aspects of effective advocates.

13.2.2 Innovation

Innovation is a key way in which individuals and communities can participate in shaping the future of environmental leadership. By developing new ideas, approaches, and technologies, we can create more sustainable and equitable systems that benefit both people and the planet.

There are many areas where innovation can make a significant impact on environmental sustainability. For example, developing new renewable energy technologies can help to reduce our reliance on fossil fuels and promote the transition to a low-carbon economy. Similarly, creating more sustainable agricultural practices can help to reduce the environmental footprint of food production and increase resilience in agricultural systems.

Innovation can also involve the rethinking of existing systems and practices to find more sustainable and efficient ways of doing things. For example, using circular economy principles to redesign product and material flows can help to minimize waste and maximize resource efficiency.

13.2.3 Collaboration

Collaboration is an essential component of shaping the future of environmental leadership. By building networks and coalitions with other individuals and organizations, we can amplify our impact and create more effective solutions to complex environmental challenges.

Effective collaboration involves working across sectors and disciplines to develop innovative approaches to sustainability and environmental justice. This can involve engaging in ongoing dialogue and collaboration with stakeholders from a diverse range of backgrounds, including government, academia, industry, and civil society.

Key benefits of collaboration include increased knowledge sharing, improved coordination and alignment of efforts, and greater leverage and impact. By working together, we can create more powerful and effective solutions to environmental challenges that benefit both people and the planet.

Collaboration also helps to build stronger and more resilient communities that are better equipped to address environmental challenges over the long term. By fostering relationships and partnerships across sectors and disciplines, we can create a more inclusive and equitable approach to environmental leadership that prioritizes the needs and perspectives of all stakeholders.

13.3 Staying Hopeful, Curious, and Creative in the Face of Uncertainty and Complexity

Environmental sustainability is a complex and ever-evolving challenge, and it can be easy to become discouraged in the face of the many uncertainties and obstacles that we face. However, staying hopeful, curious, and creative is essential to maintaining momentum and driving progress towards a more sustainable future.

One key challenge associated with environmental sustainability is the sheer complexity of the issues we face. Environmental problems are often interconnected, and their solutions require a holistic understanding of social, economic, and political systems. This can make it challenging to identify effective solutions and to maintain momentum in the face of ongoing challenges.

To stay hopeful, curious, and creative in the face of these challenges, it is important to cultivate a mindset of resilience and adaptability. This involves acknowledging the uncertainty and complexity of environmental issues, while also remaining open to new ideas and approaches.

13.3.1 Embrace Innovation

Embracing innovation is an essential strategy for staying hopeful, curious, and creative when it comes to environmental sustainability. It involves being open to new ideas and approaches, and being willing to experiment with new solutions and technologies.

Innovation provides us with the opportunity to develop more effective approaches to environmental problem-solving that are both sustainable and equitable. Whether it involves developing new renewable energy technologies, designing more efficient waste management systems, or creating more sustainable agricultural practices, innovation has the power to drive progress towards a more sustainable and just future.

Key strategies for embracing innovation include fostering a culture of curiosity and inquiry, encouraging experimentation and risk-taking, and promoting cross-disciplinary collaboration. By prioritizing these strategies, we can create a more dynamic and innovative approach to environmental leadership that is grounded in creativity and exploration.

Embracing innovation also requires us to be aware of and responsive to emerging trends and innovations in the field of environmental sustainability. This can involve staying informed about the latest research and best practices, attending conferences and workshops, and engaging with experts and thought leaders in the field.

By embracing innovation, we can create more adaptive, resilient, and sustainable systems that benefit both people and the planet. We can develop new solutions to complex environmental challenges and promote a more sustainable and just future for all.

13.3.2 Focus on Collaboration

Focusing on collaboration and community building is another essential strategy for staying hopeful, curious, and creative when it comes to environmental sustainability. It involves working together with others who share our passion and commitment to environmental sustainability, to create powerful networks and coalitions that can drive real change.

Effective collaboration involves working collaboratively towards common goals, leveraging the strengths and expertise of all partners involved. This can involve pooling resources, sharing knowledge and insights, and engaging in ongoing communication and dialogue.

Key benefits of collaboration include increased leverage and impact, improved coordination and alignment of efforts, and the ability to tackle complex environmental challenges that no single organization or individual can address alone.

Collaboration can take many different forms, from formal collaborations between organizations to informal networks of individuals working towards a shared vision. Regardless of their form, effective collaborations are characterized by a shared commitment to sustainability and environmental justice, as well as a willingness to listen, learn, and collaborate.

Focusing on collaboration and community building also helps us to build stronger and more resilient communities that are better equipped to address environmental challenges over the long term. By fostering relationships and partnerships across sectors and disciplines, we can create a more inclusive and equitable approach to environmental leadership that prioritizes the needs and perspectives of all stakeholders.

13.3.3   Be Adaptable

Being adaptable and resilient is an essential mindset for driving progress towards a more sustainable future. Environmental problem-solving is complex, and it often involves navigating a variety of challenges and setbacks. Cultivating a mindset of resilience and adaptability helps us to stay focused and motivated, even in the face of adversity.

One key element of resilience and adaptability is being able to learn from failures and setbacks. When we encounter obstacles or challenges, it is important to take the time to reflect on what we can learn from the experience and how we can use that learning to inform our future actions. By embracing a growth mindset and being willing to learn from mistakes, we can continue to innovate and develop effective solutions to complex environmental challenges.

Another important element of resilience and adaptability is the ability to remain flexible and open to new ideas and approaches. This means being willing to shift strategies or pivot in response to changing circumstances, while staying true to our core values and commitments. By remaining flexible and adaptable, we can respond more effectively to emerging challenges and opportunities, and continue to drive progress towards a more sustainable future.

Finally, building resilience and adaptability also involves cultivating a strong support network, including partners, colleagues, and mentors who can provide guidance and support when we need it most. By working collaboratively and building strong relationships with others, we can create a more supportive and resilient community, and improve our own leadership skills.

13.4 Case Studies in Future-oriented Environmental Leadership

Case studies of successful future-oriented environmental leadership initiatives can provide valuable insights into effective approaches to environmental problem-solving. Here are a few examples of successful initiatives:

13.4.1 The Circular Innovation City

The Circular Innovation City is an initiative in multiple large cities that seeks to create a more sustainable and circular city by developing innovative solutions for waste reduction, recycling, and resource efficiency. The initiative involves collaboration between businesses, government agencies, and academic institutions, and has resulted in the development of new technologies, policies, and business models that promote sustainability and circularity.

Lessons learned: Collaboration and innovation are key to driving progress towards more sustainable and circular systems. Multi-stakeholder partnerships can help to break down silos and foster new approaches to problem-solving.

13.4.2 The Green New Deal

The Green New Deal is a policy framework that has gained traction in the United States and other countries as a way to address environmental challenges while also promoting social and economic equity. The framework calls for investments in green infrastructure, renewable energy, and sustainable agriculture, as well as initiatives to promote social justice and job creation.

Lessons learned: Environmental sustainability and social equity are closely connected, and addressing both of these issues is essential to creating a more just and sustainable future. Even if these proposed policies never become law, progressive policy frameworks can be powerful tools for driving change.

13.4.3 The Plastics Pact

The Plastics Pact is a global initiative that brings together businesses, governments, and NGOs to reduce plastic waste and pollution. The initiative includes commitments to reduce plastic use, increase recycling rates, and promote innovation in sustainable packaging.

Lessons learned: Addressing the challenge of plastic waste requires collaboration and innovation across sectors and industries. Business-led initiatives can be powerful drivers of change, but they must be grounded in rigorous science and environmental principles.

These case studies demonstrate that effective future-oriented environmental leadership requires collaboration, innovation, and a commitment to sustainability and equity. In learning from these examples, we can develop new approaches and strategies for addressing the complex environmental challenges we face, and continue to make progress towards a more sustainable and just future.

13.5 CHALLENGES AND SOLUTIONS

Envisioning the future of environmental leadership is a complex and ever-evolving challenge, and there are several common challenges that can arise. These challenges include the complexity and interconnectedness of environmental issues, the pace of technological change, the need for collaboration and innovation across sectors, and the urgency of addressing urgent environmental challenges such as climate change and biodiversity loss.

13.5.1 Continuous Learning

To overcome the challenges facing environmental leadership and stay adaptable in the face of uncertainty and complexity, it is important to embrace a mindset of continuous learning and growth. This involves staying informed about emerging trends and innovations in environmental leadership and being open to new ideas and approaches.

Continuous learning can take many different forms, from attending conferences and workshops to engaging in online learning and self-directed study. By staying current with the latest research and best practices in environmental leadership, we can gain new insights and perspectives that can help us to adapt and innovate in response to changing circumstances.

Key strategies for continuous learning include networking and collaboration, seeking out diverse perspectives and experiences, and being open to feedback and critique. By prioritizing these strategies, we can create a more dynamic and responsive approach to environmental leadership that is grounded in ongoing learning and growth.

13.5.2   Partnership

Partnership is a critical strategy for overcoming challenges in environmental leadership. By working together with others who share our passion and commitment to environmental sustainability, we can create powerful networks and coalitions that can drive real change.

Effective partnerships involve working collaboratively towards common goals, leveraging the strengths and expertise of all partners involved. This can involve pooling resources, sharing knowledge and insights, and engaging in ongoing communication and dialogue.

Key benefits of partnerships include increased leverage and impact, improved coordination and alignment of efforts, and the ability to tackle complex environmental challenges that no single organization or individual can address alone.

Partnerships can take many different forms, from formal collaborations between organizations to informal networks of individuals working towards a shared vision. Regardless of their form, effective partnerships are characterized by a shared commitment to sustainability and environmental justice, as well as a willingness to listen, learn, and collaborate.

13.5.3 Creativity

Creativity is an essential element of environmental leadership. By embracing innovation and creativity, we can develop new ideas, approaches, and technologies that can help us to create more sustainable and equitable systems that benefit both people and the planet.

Whether it involves developing new renewable energy technologies, creating more sustainable agricultural practices, or designing innovative solutions to waste reduction and management, creativity has the power to drive progress towards a more sustainable future.

Key strategies for fostering creativity include encouraging experimentation and risk-taking, creating opportunities for cross-disciplinary collaboration, and promoting a culture of curiosity and inquiry. By prioritizing these strategies, we can create a more dynamic and innovative approach to environmental leadership that is grounded in creativity and exploration.

Creativity can also help to foster greater engagement and participation among diverse stakeholders, including those who may not have traditionally been involved in environmental issues. By creating more engaging and interactive experiences that tap into people's creativity and imagination, we can foster greater public support and investment in environmental sustainability.

13.5.4   DEI

Creativity is an essential element of environmental leadership. By embracing innovation and creativity, we can develop new ideas, approaches, and technologies that can help us to create more sustainable and equitable systems that benefit both people and the planet.

Whether it involves developing new renewable energy technologies, creating more sustainable agricultural practices, or designing innovative solutions to waste reduction and management, creativity has the power to drive progress towards a more sustainable future.

Key strategies for fostering creativity include encouraging experimentation and risk-taking, creating opportunities for cross-disciplinary collaboration, and promoting a culture of curiosity and inquiry. By prioritizing these strategies, we can create a more dynamic and innovative approach to environmental leadership that is grounded in creativity and exploration.

Creativity can also help to foster greater engagement and participation among diverse stakeholders, including those who may not have traditionally been involved in environmental issues. By creating more engaging and interactive experiences that tap into people's creativity and imagination, we can foster greater public support and investment in environmental sustainability.

13.6 INNOVATIONS IN ENVIRONMENTAL LEADERSHIP

In, the future of environmental leadership is characterized by emerging trends and innovations that respond to the complex challenges of sustainability in a rapidly changing world. These include regenerative design, circular economy, social entrepreneurship, and citizen science, among others.

As individuals and communities, we have a crucial role to play in shaping the future of environmental leadership. By advocating for policies and practices that promote sustainability and environmental justice, embracing innovation and creativity, and working collaboratively with others, we can create more sustainable and equitable systems that benefit both people and the planet.

It is essential to remain hopeful, curious, and resilient in the face of the challenges and uncertainties of environmental problem-solving, and to embrace a mindset of continuous learning and growth. In staying informed about emerging trends and innovations, we drive progress towards a better future.

13.7 REFLECTIVE QUESTIONS

1. How can you personally contribute to shaping the future of environmental leadership?

2. What are some environmental challenges in your community that you could help to address through advocacy or collaboration with others?

3. How can you embrace a mindset of continuous learning and growth when it comes to environmental leadership?

4. What are some innovative ideas or approaches you have come across in the field of environmental sustainability?

5. How can you build stronger partnerships and networks with other individuals and organizations that share your commitment to environmental sustainability?

6. What role can creativity play in driving progress towards a more sustainable and just future?

7. What are some barriers that prevent greater public engagement and investment in environmental sustainability, and how can they be overcome?

8. How can you incorporate principles of sustainability and environmental justice into your personal and professional life?

9. What are some examples of successful environmental leadership initiatives in your region or beyond, and what can we learn from them?

10. How can you stay motivated and inspired to continue working towards a more sustainable and just future, even in the face of challenges and setbacks?

13.8 SUGGESTED ACTIVITIES

1. Attend a local environmental organization's meeting or event and learn more about their work and how you can get involved.

2. Identify an environmental challenge in your community and develop a plan for addressing it through advocacy or collaboration with others.

3. Organize a brainstorming session with friends or colleagues to generate innovative ideas and approaches to environmental sustainability and share them with your local government representatives.

14 Where To Go From Here

In this final chapter, I draw together the key insights and lessons, and explore how they can be applied to cultivate environmental leadership in ourselves and others.

The book is divided into four parts, each of which offers unique perspectives on environmental leadership and provides practical tools and strategies for developing the skills and mindset required for effective action.

In "Finding Your Why," we explored the importance of developing a clear sense of purpose and values, and how this can drive meaningful action towards a more sustainable future.

In "Filling Your Knowledge Gaps," we delved into the knowledge and skills required for effective environmental leadership, and provided practical guidance for building expertise and staying informed.

In "Walking the Walk," we explored the role of personal actions and behavior change in environmental sustainability, and offered strategies for making sustainable choices in our daily lives.

Finally, in "Becoming a Leader," we looked at the qualities and skills required for effective leadership, and offered guidance on how to build these skills in ourselves and others.

Throughout the book, I have emphasized the importance of collaboration and community building in driving progress towards a more sustainable future. Together, we have explored the power of innovation and creativity, the need for resilience and adaptability, and the importance of embracing principles of sustainability and environmental justice in all aspects of our lives.

My hope is that this book has inspired you to take action towards a more sustainable future and has provided practical guidance and support for cultivating environmental leadership in yourself and others. With the challenges facing our planet today, the need for effective environmental leadership has never been greater.

14.1 LESSONS LEARNED FROM THE BOOK

Throughout "Envisioning the Future of Environmental Leadership," we have explored a range of themes and insights related to effective environmental leadership. Some of the most important lessons we have learned include:

1. The importance of developing a clear sense of purpose and values, and how this can drive meaningful action towards a more sustainable future.

2. The value of ongoing learning and development, and the need for continuous improvement in our knowledge and skills related to environmental sustainability.

3. The key role that personal actions and behavior change play in promoting environmental sustainability, and the importance of making sustainable choices in our daily lives.

4. The importance of building strong partnerships and networks with others who share our commitment to environmental

sustainability, and the value of collaboration and community building.

5. The critical, non-negotiable nature of DEI (diversity, equity, and inclusion) in your leadership work and path.

6. The qualities and skills required for effective leadership, and how these can be developed and applied in the context of environmental sustainability.

These lessons have important implications for personal and collective action for environmental sustainability. When we cultivate a clear sense of purpose and values, and prioritize ongoing learning and development, we can drive meaningful action towards a more sustainable future. By making sustainable choices in our personal lives and building strong partnerships and networks with others, we can create powerful coalitions that can drive real change. In developing the qualities and skills required for effective leadership, we can inspire and mobilize others to take action towards a more sustainable and just world.

14.2 NEXT STEPS IN CULTIVATING ENVIRONMENTAL LEADERSHIP

As you conclude your journey through this book, it is important to recognize the importance of ongoing learning and growth in environmental leadership. The field of environmental sustainability is constantly evolving, and staying informed and up-to-date on emerging trends and best practices is essential for becoming an **effective** environmental leader.

To continue cultivating environmental leadership in yourself and others, there are a variety of strategies and tactics that you can use. These include attending conferences and workshops, participating in online courses and webinars, joining environmental organizations and networks, and engaging in ongoing reading and research. Other strategies can include volunteering for environmental initiatives, mentoring others, and seeking out feedback and constructive criticism to continuously improve your skills and approach to environmental sustainability.

In addition to these strategies, it is important to set personal goals and create accountability systems for continued progress. This can involve setting specific targets for personal behavior change, such as reducing energy consumption or waste production, or developing new initiatives or programs related to environmental sustainability. Creating accountability systems can involve partnering with others who share your commitment to these goals, or using tools such as habit trackers or progress reports to monitor and track progress over time.

Finally, it is important to recognize that cultivating environmental leadership is an ongoing process that requires continuous learning, growth, and self-reflection. Just stay engaged and committed, set personal goals, and create accountability systems for continued progress. You, too, can become a more effective environmental leader and contribute to a more sustainable future for all.

14.3 CONNECTING WITH A GLOBAL NETWORK OF ENVIRONMENTAL LEADERS

As you continue your journey towards cultivating environmental leadership, it is important to recognize the value of connecting with a global network of environmental leaders. By building relationships with like-minded individuals and organizations from around the world, you can gain inspiration, learn about new approaches and best practices, and collaborate on meaningful action towards a more sustainable future.

There are many different ways in which individuals can connect with a global network of environmental leaders. Social media platforms such as Twitter, LinkedIn, and Facebook provide opportunities to connect with other environmental leaders from around the world, share information and resources, and engage in discussions on important topics related to environmental sustainability. Additionally, attending conferences and workshops related to environmental sustainability can provide valuable opportunities for networking and collaboration with others in the field. Joining environmental organizations and networks, both locally and globally, can also help individuals connect with a diverse range of stakeholders and build relationships that can lead to meaningful action.

Building relationships with diverse stakeholders is essential for collaborative action towards a more sustainable future. By engaging with individuals and organizations from different backgrounds, cultures, and perspectives, we can develop a deeper understanding of the complex challenges facing our planet, and work together to find creative solutions that reflect diverse needs and priorities. Collaboration can lead to greater impact, bringing together the skills, knowledge, and resources of multiple stakeholders to drive transformative change on a larger scale.

Overall, connecting with a global network of environmental leaders is an important step towards becoming an effective environmental leader and driving meaningful action towards a more sustainable future. In building relationships, collaborating with others, and sharing knowledge and resources, we can create a powerful movement for change.

14.4 CONCLUSION

In conclusion, this book has explored the importance of individual and collective action for environmental sustainability, and has offered practical guidance and support for cultivating environmental leadership in ourselves and others. Through our journey together, we have learned about the power of purpose, ongoing learning and growth, personal actions and behavior change, partnerships and networks, and effective leadership in the context of environmental sustainability.

As we move forward, it is critical that we take action towards a more sustainable future. We each have a role to play in driving progress towards environmental sustainability, whether through small changes in our daily lives or larger initiatives within our communities and networks. By becoming environmental leaders, we can inspire and mobilize others to take action, and create a powerful movement for change that reflects our shared values and priorities.

I encourage readers to take the lessons learned from this book and apply them in their own lives and communities. By staying informed, setting personal goals, building partnerships, and taking meaningful action towards a more sustainable future, we can create a world that is more just, equitable, and resilient.

9 798869 231895